Better Homes and Gardens.

L·O·V·A·B·L·E
GIFTS FOR BABIES

© Copyright 1985 by Meredith Corporation, Des Moines, Iowa.
All Rights Reserved. Printed in the United States of America.
First Edition. Third Printing, 1986.
Library of Congress Catalog Card Number: 84-62406
ISBN: 0-696-01440-8 (hard cover)
ISBN: 0-696-01442-4 (trade paperback)

BETTER HOMES AND GARDENS® BOOKS

Editor: Gerald M. Knox
Art Director: Ernest Shelton
Managing Editor: David A. Kirchner

Copy and Production Editors: Marsha Jahns,
    Mary Helen Schiltz, Carl Voss, David A. Walsh

Crafts Editor: Nancy Lindemeyer
Senior Crafts Books Editor: Joan Cravens
Associate Crafts Books Editors: Laura Holtorf Collins,
    Sara Jane Treinen

Associate Art Directors: Linda Ford Vermie,
    Neoma Alt West, Randall Yontz
Assistant Art Directors: Harijs Priekulis,
    Tom Wegner
Senior Graphic Designers: Alisann Dixon,
    Lynda Haupert, Lyne Neymeyer
Graphic Designers: Mike Burns, Mike Eagleton,
    Deb Miner, Stan Sams, Darla Whipple-Frain

Vice President, Editorial Director: Doris Eby
Executive Director, Editorial Services: Duane L. Gregg

Senior Vice President, General Manager: Fred Stines
Director of Publishing: Robert B. Nelson
Vice President, Retail Marketing: Jamie Martin
Vice President, Direct Marketing: Arthur Heydendael

Lovable Gifts for Babies
Crafts Editor: Sara Jane Treinen
Contributing Crafts Editor: Gary Boling
Copy and Production Editor: David A. Walsh
Graphic Designers: Linda Ford Vermie,
    Darla Whipple-Frain
Electronic Text Processor: Donna Russell

CONTENTS

HEIRLOOM GIFTS

FROM ONE DESIGN

In many families, passing along a treasured baby gift to infants and their parents is a long-standing tradition. And when the gift is handmade, it's an extra-special gesture. Here and on following pages you'll find gifts for newborns that are sure to become keepsakes in your own family, to be cherished for years to come. Instructions and patterns for all of the projects begin on page 10.

Adorned with blue ribbons and floral appliqués, the crib quilt, *at left,* is a showcase for a good stitcher's talents. Letters are the focal points of the quilt blocks, which are bordered in calico in the manner of traditional Log Cabin quilt patterns.

Purchased flower appliqués add a delicate touch, but simple hand-embroidered flowers could be just as effective.

The ribbon border is appliquéd in a solid and a blue print fabric.

More flower appliqués accompany the ribbon, and heart outline quilting adds a sweet touch.

Borrowing the ribbons, garlands, and flower alphabet, the baby announcement, *near left,* is a beautiful sampler for a cross-stitcher. Begin by charting the baby's name and birth date in the spaces provided, and then add rows of delicate sampler motifs, including numerals, bows, birds, and various flower designs.

The inner border is another version of the flowered alphabet, set within pastel squares and borders. The graceful stitched ribbons (in two shades of blue) form the final outer border, entwined with spring flowers.

Graceful bows embellish the freestanding picture or mirror frame, *opposite.* This design is worked in cross- and half-cross-stitches over perforated paper. A scattering of stitched blossoms and a heart complete the design.

To adapt this frame design to fit a photograph of another size, work out a new design on graph paper first. Decide how large to make the center opening, and add the bow motifs at each corner. Then add the flowers along the sides, adapting or repeating the blossoms as necessary.

The design also can be embroidered onto any type or color of even-weave fabric. Or work it in continental stitches on needlepoint canvas. For best results, experiment with new materials before beginning the project.

Sturdy building blocks like the ones *at right* can last through years and years of hard play. They're made from scraps of clear pine or other softwood, and the woodburned and painted motifs and letters are adapted from the quilt and sampler on the preceding pages. Clear varnish protects the designs and makes them sparkle.

The time-honored art of smocking is put to beautiful use for the baby's bib, *above.* We chose A-B-C as the stitched letters, but you can substitute your baby's name or initials.

As an alternative, cover a crib pillow with the finished smocking, or create an extra-special photograph album cover for your newborn.

HEIRLOOM GIFTS

Bundle up a newborn in great style with the knitted Fair Isle bunting, *opposite*. It's worked in rounds from the bottom edge to the underarms with rows and rows of hearts and floral motifs. The full-length sleeves are added to the circular needles, and the yoke is shaped with decrease rounds.

The bunting is styled for a boy or girl, and features animal-shaped buttons designed especially for a baby's clothes. As the infant grows, the drawstring at the bottom can come off for greater freedom of movement.

The matching cap is knitted with the same Fair Isle motifs and has jaunty earflaps and ties to keep the cap snugly in place.

Inspired by antique Victorian garments, the christening gown and bonnet, *left* and *above*, will be treasured always. The fine batiste fabric used for both projects provides a snowy white background for the delicate embroidery, ribbon, and lace.

The bonnet brim is embroidered with bird, ribbon, and flower motifs, and is accented with pleated eyelet trim and satin ribbons.

Assemble the christening gown with a purchased pattern. The focal point of the gown is its elegant 45-inch-long lined skirt, which is made of shirred panels. The yoke and front are embroidered with some of the same motifs used on the bonnet and embellished with satin ribbon rosettes and leaves.

Appliquéd Crib Quilt

Shown on page 4.

Finished size is 40x45 inches.

MATERIALS
¼ yard of blue fabric for the appliquéd letters
¼ yard of 6 assorted fabrics for sashing strips, ribbon, and heart appliqués
1½ yards of muslin for quilt blocks and borders
1½ yards of backing fabric
Quilt batting
Purchased floral appliqués

INSTRUCTIONS
Enlarge all patterns, *right,* onto graph paper. Preshrink and press all fabrics. Transfer patterns to fabric, adding ¼-inch seam allowances to each piece.

Cut out letters, hearts, and the bow appliqués from fabrics. Cut thirty 4½-inch muslin squares. For the framing strips around all the squares, cut thirty 1x5½-inch strips from *each* of 4 fabrics.

Turn under seam allowances on letters, hearts, and bow border designs; baste. Clip curves. Sew letters and hearts on squares.

With right sides together, using the same color sequence around each block, sew the first strip to the square, allowing a 1-inch extension at bottom of this strip only. Working counterclockwise and in log-cabin style, piece the remaining 3 strips around the block. Fold back the first strip and sew the 1-inch extension over last strip. Complete all blocks before joining together.

Piece the 30 blocks in 5 rows of 6 blocks each. (Assemble squares in alphabetical order; add heart blocks in 4 corners.) Sew the rows together.

For the border, cut two strips 7¾x40½ inches and two strips 7¾x45½ inches from the muslin. Sew strips to quilt top, mitering corners. Baste and sew ribbon and bow appliqués to the borders.

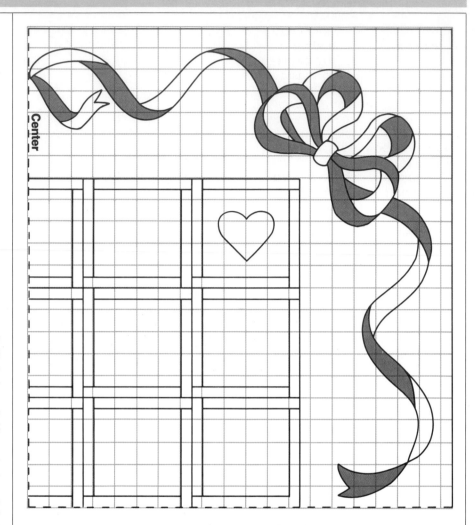

Center

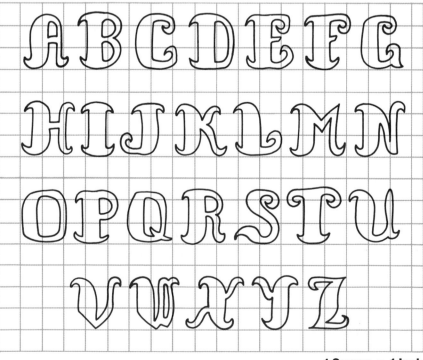

1 Square = 1 Inch

Cut backing fabric and batting 2 inches larger on all sides than quilt top. Place batting between quilt top and backing; baste all layers together. With pink quilting thread, quilt around edges of blocks and the appliquéd pieces. Quilt hearts in open spaces on borders of bow design. Remove basting threads.

Fold backing fabric over quilt top, turning raw edges under ½ inch and trimming excess fabric and batting. Hand-sew backing in place. Add purchased floral appliqués as desired to complete.

Perforated Paper Frame

Shown on page 6.

Finished size is 8x9¼ inches.

MATERIALS
Perforated paper
Embroidery floss in the following colors: peach, yellow, lavender, rose, dark and light blues, dark and light greens
Tapestry needle
Graph paper
Felt-tip pens to match floss
Artist's stretcher strips
Double-faced tape

INSTRUCTIONS
Transfer the pattern, *right,* to graph paper using marking pens that correspond with the color key. Make mirror image of diagram to complete pattern.

Staple perforated paper to artist's stretcher strips. Stitch with two strands of floss to work cross-stitches over one square of perforated paper.

Take care when stitching; constant ripping and restitching may tear the paper.

When the design is completed, cut a 3½x4-inch opening in center of paper. Slash to corners and fold edges under. Trim outside edges of paper, leaving ½ inch beyond the design; fold under. Cut a cardboard backing to match finished piece. Secure the embroidery to cardboard backing using double-faced tape.

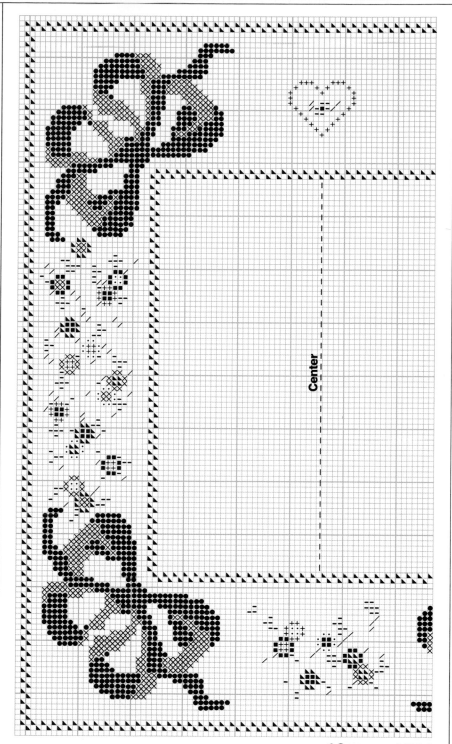

1 Square = 1 Stitch

COLOR KEY

◕ Dark blue	▪ Yellow	⊟ Light green
⊠ Light blue	⊡ Lavender	▨ Dark green
◣ Peach	⊞ Rose	

Center

Cross-Stitched Sampler

Shown on page 5.

Finished size is 18x20 inches.

MATERIALS
22x24-inch piece of white
  hardanger fabric
Embroidery floss in colors noted
  in the color key
Tapestry needle, embroidery
  hoop, felt-tip pens
Masking tape, graph paper

INSTRUCTIONS
Transfer the complete design, pages 12–15, onto graph paper using felt-tip marking pens. Use the letters and numbers on this pattern to help design your own alphabet and numbers to personalize your sampler in the space provided. If necessary, eliminate some of the design elements in the center of the chart to make your inscriptions fit. Chart your names and dates onto the graph paper *before* stitching.

Bind the edges of the fabric with the masking tape. Use two strands of floss to work over two fabric threads. Determine the center of the design and the fabric; begin stitching here.

Mount the fabric in the hoop and begin cross-stitching. Make a stitch that slants from the lower right to the upper left. Work back across the half cross-stitch with a stitch slanting from lower left to upper right. This stitching combination results in an X shape.

Work the center of the design first, then stitch the border.

Using a warm iron, press the finished sampler facedown on a damp towel. Center the sampler atop a padded mat board. Tape the edges to the back of the mat board and frame as desired.

Cross-Stitch Tips for the Wrong Side of Your Stitchery

Although the *back* of a stitchery may seem unimportant, many embroiders care about the uniformity of the stitches on the underside of their work. To make the wrong side of cross-stitched embroidery as attractive as possible, follow these suggestions:

Whenever possible, stitch so the direction of the threads on the reverse side is vertical. Accomplish this by working across a row, stitching half the crosses; then reverse the stitching to complete the cross-stitched row. (Occasionally, a horizontal stitch is unavoidable.)

When stitching with a variety of colors, you need not end your thread every time you complete a small color area. Carry the thread across the back of the fabric by slipping the threaded needle under the previously stitched crosses to the point where embroidery begins again with that color.

COLOR KEY

⊠ Light Blue
▣ Dark Blue
⊞ Light Green
◉ Dark Green
⬡ Light Peach
◪ Dark Rose
⊡ Yellow
⬙ Lavender

HEIRLOOM GIFTS

COLOR KEY

⊠	Light Blue	◨	Light Peach
◪	Dark Blue	◪	Dark Rose
⊞	Light Green	⊡	Yellow
◙	Dark Green	◩	Lavender

1 Square = 1 Stitch

HEIRLOOM GIFTS

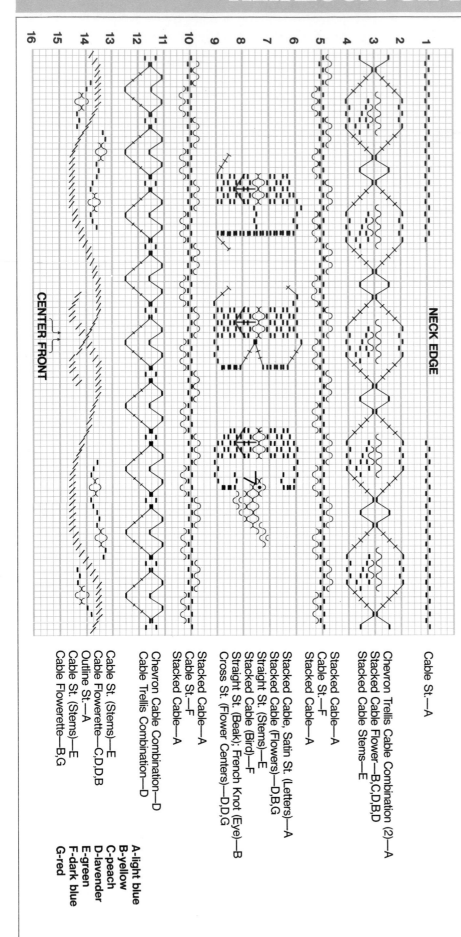

NECK EDGE

CENTER FRONT

Cable St.—A

Chevron Trellis Cable Combination (2)—A
Stacked Cable Flower—B,C,D,B,D
Stacked Cable Stems—E

Stacked Cable—A
Cable St.—F
Stacked Cable—A

Stacked Cable, Satin St. (Letters)—A
Stacked Cable (Flowers)—D,B,G
Straight St. (Stems)—F
Stacked Cable (Bird)—F
Straight St. (Beak); French Knot (Eye)—B
Cross St. (Flower Centers)—D,D,G

Stacked Cable—A
Cable St.—F
Stacked Cable—A

Chevron Cable Combination—D
Cable Trellis Combination—D

Cable St. (Stems)—E
Cable Flowerette—C,D,D,B
Outline St.—A
Cable St. (Stems)—E
Cable Flowerette—B,G

A-light blue
B-yellow
C-peach
D-lavender
E-green
F-dark blue
G-red

Smocked Bib

Shown on page 7.

MATERIALS
Pleating machine (or iron-on dots) for gathering fabric
¼ yard white cotton fabric
½ yard print backing fabric
Embroidery floss in colors cited in color key, *left*
Water-erasable pen
1 yard narrow cotton cording
1 yard white double-fold bias tape

INSTRUCTIONS
From white fabric, cut a strip measuring 7x24 inches. Pleat 16 basting rows to measure 5 inches across. Back-smock on the wrong side of piece.

Begin smocking at center on *front.* Follow chart, *left,* for embroidery. When smocking is complete, *steam* pleats. Remove basting threads. Stretch piece to measure 5 inches wide. Transfer neckline and curved bottom edges to the smocked piece with water-erasable pen.

Enlarge bib pattern, *below,* onto graph paper and transfer to printed fabric adding ⅜-inch seam allowance; cut pieces. Make a 30-inch strip of piping from printed fabric; sew it to right side of outside edge of smocked inset.

Turn under seam allowance on inside curved edge of front border piece and sew in place to smocked inset section along piping strip.

Sew remaining piping strip to outside edge of bib front. With right sides facing, sew front to back, leaving neckline edge open. Clip curves and turn; press. Trim excess fabric along neckline edge. Sew bias tape to neckline and finish ends for ties.

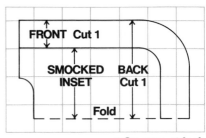

FRONT Cut 1

SMOCKED INSET   BACK Cut 1

Fold

1 Square = 1 Inch

Wood Blocks

Shown on page 7.

Finished block is 5 inches square.

MATERIALS
Scraps of 1-inch pine
Wood glue; carbon paper
No. 4 finishing nails
Wood filler; sandpaper
Woodburning tools
Acrylic paints; varnish

INSTRUCTIONS
From pine, cut 4 side pieces, each 4¼x5 inches, and top and bottom, each 3½x3½ inches.

Using glue and nails, butt-join the sides to the top and bottom. Fill nail holes with wood filler; sand.

Using patterns from quilt on page 10 as a guide, make patterns of letters and flowers to fit block. Transfer designs to sides, top, and bottom of block using carbon paper. Then woodburn outlines of shapes. On the sides *only,* woodburn a narrow line border. Using acrylics, paint designs as desired; varnish to complete.

Christening Gown

Shown on page 9.

MATERIALS
Christening gown pattern (we used Folkwear Victorian Gown pattern No. 228)
1½ yards *each* of ¼-inch-wide peach and white satin ribbons
3½ yards of ⅛-inch-wide green satin ribbon
2½ yards of 1½-inch-wide eyelet beading
4 yards of ½-inch-wide gathered eyelet
Peach, lavender, light and dark green embroidery floss
Water-erasable pen

Note: Follow instructions for the above pattern, except substitute eyelet trims and ribbons as cited in materials list above for lace and ribbon notions on pattern. Our gown omits optional entredeux.

Ribbon ties at neck and waistband substitute for buttonholes.

INSTRUCTIONS
With water-erasable pen, transfer design, *below,* to the fabric yoke of pattern. Work embroidery before cutting piece. Using two strands of floss, work satin, outline, and French-knot stitches.

Weave the ¼-inch-wide green ribbon through the eyelet beading; embellish this eyelet with touches of embroidery.

Sew christening gown according to pattern instructions, substituting the ½-inch gathered and beaded eyelets for the lace. Sew beaded eyelet at the waist after the gown is assembled. Make ribbon rosettes and leaves for additional embellishments.

Rosettes (make 18): Cut peach ribbon into 2½-inch lengths. Sew ends together, making a circle. Run a gathering thread around one edge of circle. Gather ribbon into a small flower.

Leaves (make 18): Cut ⅛-inch green ribbon into 2-inch lengths. Fold ribbon into figure 8. Tack lapped areas of ribbon and sew behind rosettes.

Tack the rosettes and leaves onto gown, referring to the photograph, page 9, as a guide. With the lavender floss, stitch French knots in center of flowers.

Embroidered Baby Bonnet

Shown on page 9.

MATERIALS
½ yard *each* of white cotton blend fabric and light interfacing
½ yard of narrow flat lace trim
1 yard of 1-inch-wide gathered or pleated lace or eyelet trim
1 yard of white satin ribbon
Embroidery floss in assorted pastel colors
Small decorative beads
Water-erasable pen

INSTRUCTIONS
Enlarge patterns, page 18, onto graph paper; transfer *outline* of pattern pieces to fabric. Do not cut out front brim until design is embroidered.

Transfer embroidery design to the fabric using water-erasable pen. With two strands of floss and colors of your choice, work the design using following stitches: long and short stitches for birds; satin stitches for leaves, heart, and bow; bullion stitches for flower petals; French knots for flower centers; outline stitches for remaining embroidery. Add beads where small dots are on pattern.
continued

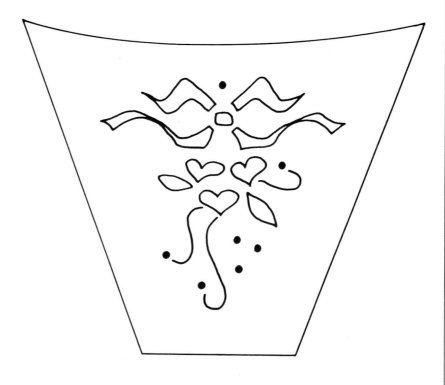

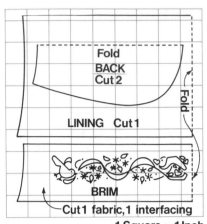

1 Square = 1 Inch

Cut the fabric pieces. Baste embroidered strip to interfacing.

Cut a 44x3-inch rectangle from the lining fabric; gather along both of the long sides until length is same as embroidered strip.

With right sides facing, sew shirred section to one edge of embroidered strip using a ⅜-inch seam. Sew narrow lace on right side behind embroidered band.

With right sides facing, baste 1-inch gathered (pleated) eyelet to front edge of embroidered strip. Right sides facing, baste a second eyelet strip to back edge of shirred fabric piece. Baste eyelet between the ⅝-inch seam allowances on both sides of two edges. Finish raw edges of the eyelet trim.

With right sides facing, pin the bonnet back to the back of the shirred strip, matching center and ends; baste. Stitch with ⅝-inch seam. Trim and clip all curves.

Make lining by joining bonnet back and lining.

With right sides facing, pin lining to bonnet. Sew front and sides, leaving an opening at lower back edge. Trim seams; turn; sew opening closed. Cut and sew on ribbon ties.

Fair-Isle Baby Bunting
Shown on page 8.

MATERIALS
Brunswick Fore-n-aft sport-weight yarn (2 ounce balls): five of ecru (MC); one *each* of cherry, peach, light blue, dark blue, mint, green, lilac, and yellow
Size 3 straight needles; 16-inch circular needle
Size 4 straight and double pointed needles; 16-inch and 24-inch circular needles
One large stitch holder, 2 small stitch holders
Nine ½-inch diameter buttons

Abbreviations: See page 47.
Gauge: 6 sts = 1 inch on Size 4 needles

INSTRUCTIONS
Note: Shaded portions of charts indicate pattern repeats. Begin pattern as shown on chart, then work repeats (shaded areas) across row, end last stitches as shown on the chart (unshaded area) to maintain mirror images of pattern along buttonhole edges.

BODY: With Size four 24-inch circular needle and MC, cast on 186 sts. Do not join. Work 6 rows in st st.
Row 7 (turning row for hem): K 1, * k 2 tog, yo, rep from * across, end k 1.
Rows 8, 10, and 12: Purl.
Rows 9 and 11: Knit. Increase 1 st on last row—187 sts.
Working in st st, work 9 rows of Chart 1, *opposite.* Work 8 rows of Chart 2. Work 17 rows of Chart 3. Rep 17 rows of Chart 3, alternating rows of flowers and hearts

until 8 rows of flowers and 7 rows of hearts are completed. Work 5 rows of MC after last row of flowers, ending with p row.
Dividing row: K 40 sts of right front and sl to holder; cast off next 10 sts for right underarm; k 87 sts for back and sl to large holder; cast off next 10 sts for left underarm; k last 40 sts for left front and sl to holder. Set body aside.

SLEEVES: With Size 3 straight needles and MC, cast on 34 sts.
Row 1: * K 1 through back lp (tbl), p 1, rep from * across. Rep this row until ribbing measures 1½ inches; inc 10 sts evenly spaced across last row—44 sts. Change to Size 4 straight needles, work 2 rows MC than work in pat as for body beginning with Chart 1 until there are 2 rows of flowers and 1 row of hearts. Keeping pat even and *at the same time,* increase 1 st at beg and end of row every fourth row 4 times—52 sts.
Work 4 more rows of MC. Cast off 5 sts at the beg of the next 2 rows. Sl remaining 42 sts on holder. Work second sleeve as for first.

YOKE: With right side facing and 24-inch circular needle, k 40 sts of right front, 42 right sleeve sts, 87 back sts, 42 left sleeve sts, 40 left front sts—251 sts. Do not join. Purl next row, decreasing 8 sts evenly spaced—243 sts. Work Chart 1 and rows 1 through 6 of Chart 2, decreasing 9 sts evenly spaced on last row—234 sts. Work Chart 4. Work 2 rows even in MC.
First neck dec row: With MC, * k 1, k 2 tog, rep from * across—156 sts. Work 6 rows of Chart 5, decrease 6 sts evenly spaced on last row—150 sts. Work Chart 6. K 1 row MC.

Center Fold

Second neck dec row: * P 1, p 2 tog, rep from * across—100 sts. Work rows 3 and 4 of Chart 2. Work 1 row MC.

Third neck dec row: * P 1, p 2 tog, rep from * across row—67 sts. Change to Size 3 needle.

Row 1: * K 1 tbl, p 1. Rep from * across, end k 1 tbl.

Row 2: * P1, k 1 tbl. Rep from *, end p 1. Rep these 2 rows for 1 inch, end with wrong side row.

Turning row for hem: * K 1, yo, k 2 tog. Rep from * across row, end k 1.

Facing: Work in st st for 1 inch. Bind off loosely.

Sew sleeve seams. Join bind-off edge of sleeve to bind-off edge of body. Turn hems at neck and lower edge to wrong side; sew in place.

FRONT BAND: Working button side first, with MC and right side facing, using Size 3 circular needle, pick up 130 sts along right front edge. To form casing for cord at lower edge, pick up sts through both thicknesses of hem, leaving 2 center rows on right side of hem open by picking up *only* hem stitches. Pick up through both thicknesses on neck ribbing. Work ribbing k 1 tbl, p 1, for 3 rows.

Row 4: K 1, * yo, k 2 tog, rep from * across, end k 1.

Row 5 and 7: Purl.

Row 6: Knit.

Row 8: K 1, * yo, k 2 tog, rep from * across, end k 1.

Rows 9-11: Work as for first 3 rows of front band. Bind off.

SECOND BAND: Make as for first band through Row 5.

Row 6 (buttonhole row): K 4 *, bind off 2 sts, k 13. Rep from * 7 times more, bind off 2 sts, end k 4.

Row 7: Purl, casting on 2 sts above bind off sts of previous row. Complete as for rows 8 through 11 for first band.

HAT: With MC and Size 3 circular needle cast on 90 sts, place marker; join work.

Row 1: * K 1 tbl, p 1. Rep from * around. *Row 2:* * K 1, p 1 tbl. Rep from * around. Rep these 2 rows for 2¼ inches.

Next row: Work ribbing over 12 sts, k next 16 sts (this forms a ridge for ear flap to be attached to); work ribbing over 34 sts, k next 16 sts, ribbing over 12 sts. Resume rib pattern and rib around until piece measures 4½ inches from beg. Change to Size four 16-inch circular needle and k 4 rnds. Work Chart 3. Rep rows 1 and 2 of Chart 3. Work 4 rounds even, decreasing 2 sts evenly spaced on last round—88 sts. Work 5 rnds of Chart 1.

Crown: Dec as follows, continuing in pattern where possible.

Rnd 1: * K 9, k 2 tog, rep from * around—80 sts. Break off lilac.

Rnd 2: * K 8, k 2 tog, rep from * around—72 sts.

Rnd 3: Alternating green and yellow, * k 7, k 2 tog, rep from * around—64 sts. Break off yellow.

Rnd 4: Change to Size 4 dp needles. Alternating green and ecru * k 6, k 2 tog, rep from * around— 56 sts. Break off green. Continue with MC and work next 6 rnds as follows:

Rnd 5: K 5, k 2 tog, rep from * around.

Rnd 6: * K 4, k 2 tog, rep from * around.

Rnd 7: * K 3, k 2 tog, rep from * around. *Rnd 8:* * K 2, k 2 tog, rep from * around.

Rnd 9: * K 1, k 2 tog, rep from * around.

Rnd 10: * K 2 tog, rep from * around—8 sts. Break off MC leaving an 8-inch end. Run end through remaining sts and draw up tightly. Fasten off.

EAR FLAP: Pick up 17 sts along purl ridge in center of ribbing. Work in garter st for 8 rows.

Row 9: K 2 tog, k to last 3 sts, k 2 tog, k 1.

Row 10: Knit. Rep last 2 rows until 5 sts remain. Work even in garter st until tie measures 4 inches. *Next row:* K 1, slip 1, k 2 tog, psso, k 1. Cast off rem sts, fasten off. Rep for other ear flap.

Make a rope cord 43 inches long. Tie knot at each end and fringe ends. Draw cord through casing at lower edge.

Make 2-inch-diameter pompom from MC, mint, cherry, and light blue. Attach to top of hat.

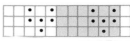

CHART 6

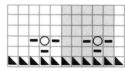

CHART 5

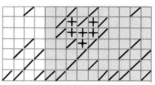

CHART 4

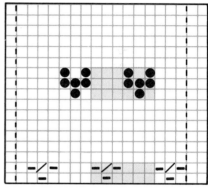

CHART 3

On body, work between solid lines. On sleeves, work between dotted lines. On hat, begin on solid line (right), end at dotted line, (left).

Row 4
Row 3

CHART 2

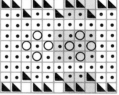

CHART 1

COLOR KEY

⊡	Yellow	⊞	Peach
☐	Ecru	⊟	Mint
▣	Blue	◣	Green
⊠	Dark Blue	◪	Lilac
⧄	Coral		

SIMPLE-TO-STITCH

PRESENTS FOR SHOWERS

♦♦♦

Showers are special occasions for family and friends to celebrate a new birth. We've assembled some extra-special gifts, and each is sure to be the hit of the party! For instructions for the projects on these four pages, turn to page 24.

Bits and pieces of colorful fabrics are put to good use for the lively bibs, *right.* Use our patterns (for a clown suit, pleated tuxedo shirt, coveralls, and shirt and tie), or create your own machine-appliquéd design. The bibs have a terry-cloth lining for softness and washable vinyl for protection. Strips of striped seersucker, cut on the bias, form the edging and ties.

A colorful string of crib toys decorates the front of the photograph album, *left.* Each toy is hand-appliquéd from calico, and tied together with a length of fabric-covered cord. The appliqué is used to cover a photo album, but would work as well as a crib pillow or framed picture.

Soft and cuddly, the bluebird toy, *below,* is fun to stitch from acrylic plush. The body parts are cut from simple shapes, and the wings are attached only at their base for extra dimension. Use felt for the eyes, and glue them to the head to make the toy safe enough for the youngest baby.

The jolly chap, *above,* is a crib toy inspired by a jack-in-the-box. His face is embroidered, and his costume is lavish enough for any funnyman. His calico home is trimmed with an initial and rickrack.

As charming as a cozy cottage can be, the three-dimensional stitchery, *right,* is a sweet addition to a nursery. Not only is it a lovely piece of sculpture, but tucked inside the cottage is a wind-up music box.

Decorating the cottage is a variety of notions, including rows of gathered lace for the thatched roof, floral satin ribbon for the beams, and narrow satin ribbon to outline the windows. An assortment of tacked-on flowers forms the lush garden.

Patterned after ordinary paper bags, the fabric gift bags, *left,* can later become handy storage containers in the nursery. The contrasting linings are secured in place with fusible webbing, and an appliquéd critter decorates the front.

The pairs of booties, *right,* can be made as plain or as fancy as you like. They work up quickly with only the simplest of sewing techniques, and can be decorated with lazy daisy embroidery stitches or perhaps a tiny embroidered initial. Add plaid or grosgrain ribbon ties. As an alternative, stitch the booties from scraps of synthetic suede.

ABCDEF GHIJKL MNOPQRSTUV WXYZ

CHILDREN ARE THE FLOWERS OF OUR LIFE

Created especially for cross-stitchers, the lively sampler, *left*, features a timeless sentiment and a stitched string of paper doll figures. Accompanying the alphabet and motto are rows of flower and border patterns that can be stitched alone on even-weave fabric to embellish towels, bibs, or other small items.

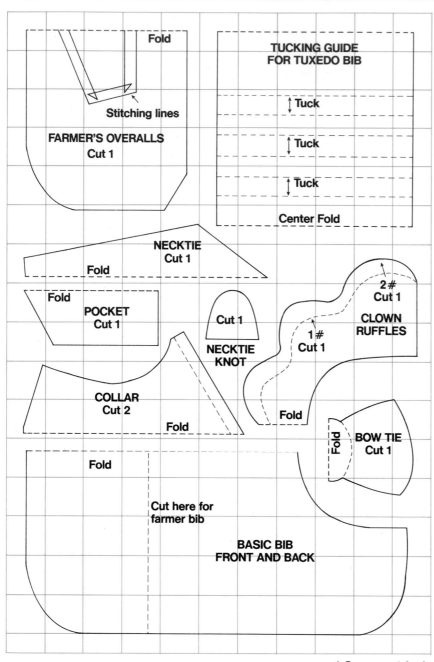

1 Square = 1 Inch

INSTRUCTIONS

BASIC INSTRUCTIONS: For the bib fronts, follow directions below. Patterns include ¼-inch seam allowances.

To assemble, cut basic bib pattern from terry cloth and vinyl. Pin together the decorated bib front (right side up), lining, and terry cloth; baste around edges.

To bind edges, use purchased bias tape or make two 1½x32-inch bias strips of seersucker. Sew one piece of tape around outer edge of bib. Center and sew other piece around neck edge. Turn under tie ends and finish.

For the necktie bib

Cut basic bib and pocket from shirting. Turn under top edge of pocket and topstitch. Press under outer edges of pocket; topstitch to left side of bib.

Cut necktie pieces. Press under long edges; machine-appliqué to bib shirt. Repeat for tie knot.

With right sides facing, fold collar on fold line; sew on dotted line. Trim corners, turn, and press. Topstitch along neckline. Follow basic directions to complete.

For the tuxedo bib

Cut a 10½x14½-inch piece of white cotton. Match center of fabric to center of tucking guide; trace tucking lines onto fabric. Press under tucks on each side; topstitch in place. Cut a 1¼x7½-inch white strip for buttonhole band. Turn under seam allowances; topstitch to center front.

Cut bib shape from the tucked piece and two collar pieces from remaining white fabric. To make collar, sew along dotted line; trim, turn, and press. Topstitch collar to neck edge.

Cut bow tie. Turn under raw edges; machine-appliqué in place. With a contrasting thread, zigzag around the inner circle.

For the buttons, cut three 1-inch-diameter circles. Gather the edges, tucking in fiberfill. Sew buttons to front panel. Follow basic directions to complete.

For the clown bib

Cut out bib shape. Cut ruffles from polka-dot fabrics. Turn un-

Baby Bibs

Shown on pages 20-21.

MATERIALS
For each bib
10½-inch squares of terry cloth and vinyl or washable plastic
¼ yard of cotton seersucker
For the necktie bib
6x12 inches of white cotton
Scrap of plaid cotton fabric for necktie
10x12 inches of striped shirting

For the tuxedo bib
12x20 inches of white fabric
Scrap of black fabric
Fiberfill; water-erasable pen
For the clown bib
10-inch square of striped fabric
Scraps of 2 polka-dot fabrics
3 purchased yarn pompoms
For the farmer bib
12-inch square of fabric with fruit or vegetable design
8x10 inches of denim
2 strawberry appliqués (buttons for overalls)
Scraps of red fabric; fiberfill

der raw edges of scalloped edges. Appliqué lower, then upper ruffle to bib; add pom-poms. Follow basic instructions to complete.

For the farmer bib

For the shirt, cut bib as shown on pattern. Cut a 1x4-inch piece from same fabric for buttonhole tab; press under long edges and topstitch in place.

Cut overalls from denim. Cut two 1½x7-inch straps. Press under long edges of straps and top of overalls. Position the overalls and straps on bib shirt; sew in place. Topstitch outline of front pocket.

For buttons, cut three 1-inch-diameter circles from red fabric. Gather edges, tucking in fiberfill; sew to front panel. To finish, follow basic instructions.

Photograph Album

Shown on page 20.

MATERIALS
Purchased album book
Plaid fabric to cover book
Fabrics for appliqués and cording
Purchased floral appliqués
16 inches narrow cotton cording
Embroidery floss as desired
Batting; water-erasable pen
Dressmaker's carbon paper
Tracing paper

INSTRUCTIONS

For the album cover
To make pattern, draw a rectangle the length of album and width of circumference (from flap to flap) onto brown paper, adding ½-inch seam allowances. Draw another rectangle for the pockets onto brown paper, the length and width of *front cover* only, adding ½-inch seam allowances.

From plaid fabric, cut 2 large and 2 small rectangles. Cut 1 large rectangle from batting.

Hem one vertical side edge on each of the smaller rectangles. With right sides facing, place one hemmed rectangle atop one end of the large rectangle, raw edges even. Repeat instructions for the other hemmed rectangle on the other edge of the large rectangle. Baste around.

Stack pieces in the following order: batting, large rectangle with pockets facing up, and the remaining large rectangle, wrong side facing up. Stitch all layers together, leaving an opening for turning. Clip corners, turn, and press. Blind-stitch opening closed. Insert album into pockets of cover.

For the appliquéd design
Enlarge the pattern, *below,* onto graph paper. Center and transfer design to the front of fabric album cover using dressmaker's carbon. With water-erasable pen, write name of baby and birth date in center of beaded necklace. Using two strands of embroidery floss and working outline stitches, embroider name and date.

Trace patterns for the appliqués. Add ¼-inch seam allowances and cut shapes from fabrics. Cover cotton cording with fabric. Embellish the appliqués with satin or running stitches. Turn under seam allowances and stitch in place. *At the same time,* attach the cording to the bead appliqués and tack in place. Embroider outline stitches around shapes. Complete by adding purchased appliqués atop the designs and stitching a double row of running stitches around outside edges of front cover ½ inch from borders.

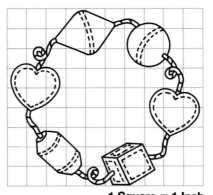

1 Square = 1 Inch

Clown Block

Shown on page 21.

MATERIALS
3x36-inch strip of fabric for body
Scraps of contrasting fabric for hat and strips outlining block
6x36-inch strip of organdy
Narrow rickrack
Scraps of white and purple felt for hands, head, and shoes
1 yard *each* of four ⅛-inch-wide pastel satin ribbons
6–10 inches of grosgrain ribbon
1-inch-diameter foam ball
Scraps of yarn for hair and tassel
Red and black embroidery floss
Polyester fiberfill

INSTRUCTIONS
Patterns, except hands and feet, include ¼-inch seam allowance.

For the body
Trace patterns, page 26. From body fabric, cut five 3x3-inch squares, and 2 rectangles, each 3x1¾ inches. With right sides facing, sew four squares into a strip. From contrasting fabric, cut 1-inch-wide bias strips as follows: 4, each 2½ inches long; 2, each 10½-inches long. Press under raw edges, lengthwise. On right side of body seams, sew bias strips over each seam and edge these strips with rickrack.

Form a letter in center on one square with ribbon and hand-sew in place (front of the clown).

Finish fourth seam on cube; add rickrack and bias tape.

With right sides together, stitch fifth square (top of cube), leaving one side open for turning.

Whipstitch around shoes and hands, leaving opening for stuffing; stuff. Place shoes between 3-inch seam line of two rectangular pieces, right sides together; sew seam. Sew this square to body, right sides together.

Turn cube right side out, stuff; hand-sew opening closed. Sew hands to sides. Add rickrack and bias strips to top and bottom edges, easing at corners to fit.

continued

For the head

Wet a 4-inch square of white felt and shape over the foam ball. Let dry; remove ball. With 3 strands of embroidery floss, make French knots for eyes and nose; work outline stitches for mouth. Fill the "ball" with fiberfill. Wrap felt, ½ inch wide, around the bottom of head to form neck. Clip excess material below neck. Tack head to top of cube.

For the hat

Stitch hat facing to hat, right sides together. Sew hat seam and leave ⅜-inch opening at top. Turn and trim edge of brim with rickrack. Make pom-pom from yarn, leaving tying ends uncut. Slip ends of pom-pom through top of hat. Sew ends to opening to secure. Tack hat in place on head.

For the hair

With yarn, make loop stitches around the face and neckline and tack in place.

For the collar

From the organdy, cut one strip 3¼ inches wide. Fold under ¼ inch on one length of organdy. Fold under ¼ inch in the opposite direction on the other side of the length. Trim to within ⅛ inch and stitch ⅛-inch ribbons atop the trimmed edges. Fold the strip slightly less than half (do not overlap the ribbon edges). Repeat for the 2¾-inch-wide strip. Lay the folded edges atop each other; hand-gather. Tack in place.

Bluebird Toy

Shown on page 21.

MATERIALS

½ yard of blue plush acrylic fur
Scraps of fleece; fiberfill
Scraps of peach, white, turquoise, and black felt for beak and eyes
15 inches of ¾-inch-wide satin ribbon

INSTRUCTIONS

Enlarge pattern pieces, page 27, onto graph paper. (Patterns include ¼-inch seam margins.) Following direction of nap (see arrows on patterns), cut pieces from plush. Cut a 6¼-inch-diameter circle for bird bottom.

Cut two wing linings from the fleece. Cut beak and beak lining from peach felt. For eyes, cut two ⅜-inch-diameter black circles, two ½-inch-diameter turquoise circles, and two ⅝-inch-diameter white circles from felt scraps.

Sew darts in head and sides. Sew straight edge of one beak to head between dots. Sew second beak to front between dots. With right sides facing, sew together front, head, and beak pieces. Poke out beak to form point. Stitch beak lining over beak opening in back, stitching around the beak edge. Clip a small hole in the lining; stuff the beak and slip-stitch closed.

With right sides facing, stitch wings to wing linings; leave an opening. Clip curves, turn, and sew closed. Sew wings to sides.

Beginning at bottom of front/head assembly, stitch front/head to sides, pivoting at neck. Clip corners and curves. Join back and upper edges of side pieces, pivoting at center. To miter tail, lay back and upper seams together; beginning ⅝ inch from the point, sew a straight line perpendicular to the seam.

Sew bird bottom to body, leaving an opening for turning. Clip curves. Turn; stuff firmly. Slip-stitch opening closed. Add felt eyes; tack bow to neck.

Cottage Music Box

Shown on page 22.

The finished music box measures 5x5⅜x5¾ inches.

MATERIALS

Music box mechanism
12x20-inch piece of ¼ inch thick foam-core board
7x8-inch piece of lightweight *white* cardboard for roof
¼ yard peach fabric for cottage
White fabric scraps for windows and door
¼ yard polyester fleece for padding the walls
Scraps of fusible webbing
2 yards of ¼-inch-wide floral trim
2 yards of ⅛-inch-wide satin peach ribbon
2–3 yards of ¼-inch-wide satin ribbon in 2 shades of green
½ yard of ⅛-inch-wide green satin ribbon for vine
2¼ yards of ¾-inch-wide pregathered white lace for roof
3 yards of ⅝-inch-wide flat white lace with scalloped edge
Small artificial flowers
Water-erasable pen; craft glue
Craft knife and ruler; ice pick

INSTRUCTIONS

For cottage sides

Enlarge all pattern pieces, page 27, onto graph paper. Cut ends and sides of house from foam-

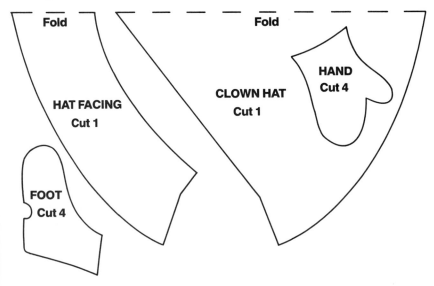

Fold

HAT FACING
Cut 1

FOOT
Cut 4

Fold

CLOWN HAT
Cut 1

HAND
Cut 4

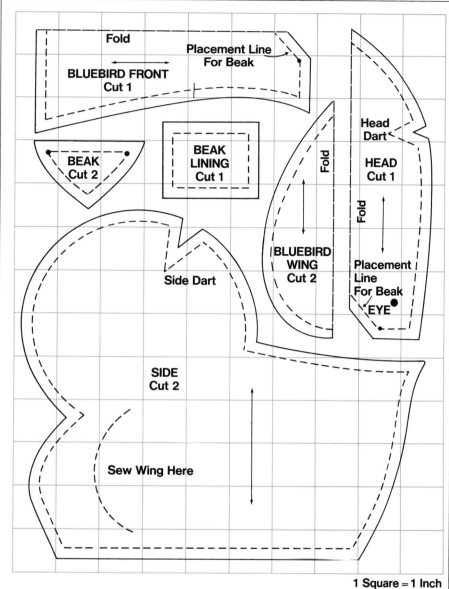

Fold

BLUEBIRD FRONT
Cut 1

Placement Line
For Beak

BEAK
Cut 2

BEAK
LINING
Cut 1

Head
Dart

HEAD
Cut 1

Fold

Fold

Side Dart

BLUEBIRD
WING
Cut 2

Placement
Line
For Beak

EYE

SIDE
Cut 2

Sew Wing Here

1 Square = 1 Inch

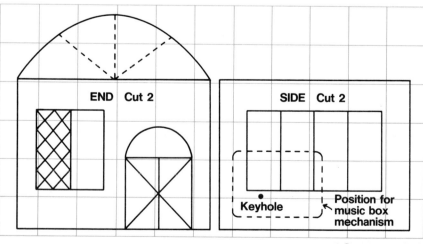

END   Cut 2

SIDE   Cut 2

Keyhole

Position for
music box
mechanism

1 Square = 1 Inch

core board. With ice pick, poke a hole for music box key on one side of cottage (dot on pattern).

Lay foam-core sides on peach fabric and draw around each shape with water-erasable pen. Cut fabric 1 inch beyond each edge.

DOOR AND WINDOWS: Trace and cut 2 large windows, 2 small windows, and door patterns onto white fabric. With fusible webbing, fuse into position on peach fabric. With water-erasable pen, divide windows into vertical sections as shown. Mark each section for ½-inch divisions. With two strands of gray thread, and using a long stitch, connect the markings in a diagonal pattern. Couch the threads at intersections with a small stitch. Glue the ⅛-inch-wide ribbon on the vertical divisions of the windows. Referring to the diagram, page 28, glue ribbon strips on door. Sew floral trim around door, gathering to fit around the curved top only.

ASSEMBLY: Cut fleece pieces the same size as the foam-core pieces and glue to each foam-core wall. Place and center foam-core, fleece side down, on wrong side of fabric pieces. Pull and glue excess fabric to back of foam-core, making sure windows are straight.

Glue the ⅛-inch-wide peach ribbon around the outside of the windows. Glue three floral trim strips and horizontal strip to top of each end of house.

Punch a hole through fabric and fleece on the side wall with key hole. Glue music box mechanism to inside of wall.

Glue end of one side wall to the inside edge of one end wall. Repeat for opposite side. Glue these two sections together.

Glue floral trim vertically along each corner edge of cottage.

Measure inside bottom dimension of cottage and cut foam-core base to fit. Glue to cottage bottom.

COTTAGE TRIMS: Run a long gathering thread down the center of the green ribbon and "squiggle" it along sides of cottage for a
continued

bushy effect. Spot-glue in place. Repeat with a second shade of green. For the vine around the door, gather the ⅛-inch-wide ribbon slightly and spot-glue. Use three separate pieces to create branches.

Glue little flowers among the ribbon bushes and vine.

For the roof

Glue lace directly onto white cardboard in alternating rows of gathered and flat lace across the 7-inch width. Glue a 9-inch strip of gathered lace across front and back edge of roof line. Glue two rows of flat lace on *underside* of front and back of roof overhang. Center roof and glue to top curved edge of cottage.

Fabric Gift Bags

Shown on page 22.

MATERIALS

⅜ yard of cotton print fabric
⅜ yard of coordinating cotton
  fabric for lining
⅜ yard of fusible interfacing
Pinking shears
Embroidery floss as desired
Scraps of fabrics and ribbons

INSTRUCTIONS

To make the bag

Preshrink the cotton fabrics. Use a paper lunch bag as a pattern. Cut the bag apart to make two pattern pieces by first cutting down the center back of the bag and then cut out the bottom. Add 1-inch seam allowance to the center back of the bag top pattern and ¼-inch seam allowance to bottom piece edges.

Cut out the bag patterns from both pieces of fabrics. With the wrong sides together, fuse the fabrics together. Overlap the 1-inch back seam allowance and fuse to join. Fold bag in half, with the lining side facing, press to make sharp folds on the two sides; stitch along both side edges

⅛ inch from the folds to within 2 inches from the bottom edges. With right sides facing, sew bottom piece to bag top; turn.

Fold the bag to establish its shape; press firmly to form the triangular lines (on sides) inward toward the lining.

Trim the top of the bag with pinking shears. Cut out the half-circle with plain shears.

To appliqué the bag

Make your own design or select one of the animal patterns, page 56, for appliqué pattern. Enlarge pattern to fit the size of the bag. Cut designs from fabric allowing ¼-inch seam allowance. Center and position appliqué approximately 1¼ inches above the bottom seam line of the bag. Embellish with embroidery and other decorative trims as desired.

Fabric Booties

Shown on page 23.

MATERIALS

4½x15-inch scrap of synthetic
  suede or felt for one pair
12 inches of ¼-inch-wide ribbon
Embroidery floss as desired
Fabric glue; pinking shears
Water-erasable pen

INSTRUCTIONS

Note: Pattern pieces include ¼-inch seam allowances.

Enlarge the pattern, *right,* onto graph paper. Cut two of each piece. Transfer the markings for the front of the upper boot and the front and back on the sole pieces with the water-erasable pen.

Work embroidery as desired on the upper boot pieces.

Mark dot for placement of ribbon ties for baby girl or slash lines for lacing for boy. Trim the top edge of the upper bootie with pinking shears. With right sides together, sew back seam of upper bootie; turn.

With the wrong sides together, stitch the upper bootie to the sole, easing to fit. Trim the edge along the sole with pinking shears.

For the girl's booties

Cut two 6-inch lengths of ribbon and position in place on the inside of the bootie. Stitch a French knot to hold in place.

For the boy's booties

With a razor blade, cut the two vertical slits on each side of the boot top. Trim the tongue with pinking shears; secure to the inside of the bootie with fabric glue. Cut two 6-inch lengths of ribbon and pull through slits for lacings.

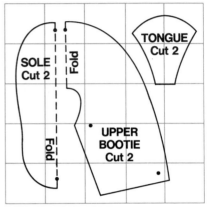

1 Square = 1 Inch

Child's Sampler

Shown on page 23.

Finished size is 12x15¾ inches.

MATERIALS

14x17-inch piece of 14-count
  Aida cloth
One skein *each* of embroidery
  floss in colors listed under the
  color key

INSTRUCTIONS

The complete design is worked in cross-stitches using two strands of floss over two threads of the Aida Cloth. Refer to page 12 for specific instructions for working the cross-stitches and the finishing details.

COLOR KEY

⊠	Light Blue	⊡	Yellow	◨	Lavender	⊞	Rose	◪	Light Green
◼	Dark Blue	⊟	Pink	◰	Peach	⊡	Flesh	◢	Dark Green

1 Square = 1 Stitch

OUACHITA TECHNICAL COLLEGE

KNIT AND CROCHET

Every baby should receive at least one set of hand-knitted booties or a crocheted crib coverlet. In this section, devoted entirely to knitters and crocheters, you'll find heirloom-quality gifts such as the layette set shown here, as well as toys, baby afghans, and other garments. Whatever your level of skill, you're sure to find a gift you'll enjoy stitching for a favorite child. Instructions for the projects begin on page 38.

Knitting a baby sweater or afghan, which calls for a smaller investment in time and materials than an adult's garment, provides a good chance to learn a new pattern or have fun with textured pattern stitches.

The layette set, *right,* is a beautiful collection of knitted pattern stitches that offers a change from cabled designs. Specialty stitches include a leaf pattern and an intricate lacy chevron motif.

Although the items could be made as an entire set, individual projects are pretty enough to be worn alone. The five-button cardigan features a deep fold-over collar and drawstring cuffs. The cap has handy earflaps and is made in a flat piece and seamed up the back. The booties, which are made mostly in garter stitches, come up well over an infant's ankles for warmth.

The two major motifs are repeated in elegant rows for the 42x36-inch afghan. Or stitch a standard-size afghan using larger needles and worsted-weight yarn.

KNIT AND CROCHET

Delightful handmade baby clothes and accessories needn't be difficult or time-consuming endeavors. The charming projects on these two pages work up quickly and are made from easy-to-find materials.

Just right for warm-weather occasions, the knitted infant dress, *opposite,* can come together easily over a weekend or two. It's made from an easy-care cotton knitting and crochet thread, with an opening along the center back, a drawstring waist, and a lacy yoke.

Although this particular dress is made from variegated thread in pastel shades, it also could be made in any solid color. For a special touch, add sweet embroidered designs across the yoke or above the hem of the dress. Or chart simple designs on graph paper and incorporate them into the dress's skirt.

The textured stitch used for the baby afghan, *above,* is a good one for beginning crocheters to master. Each of the twenty-five 6½-inch squares is worked identically and edged with rounds of double crochet.

After the squares are assembled, satin ribbon is woven through the spaces between the double crochet stitches.

A three-dimensional crocheted flower and leaf marks the intersection of the ribbon weavings.

You can use the same crocheted flower design to decorate a purchased blanket or a knitted or crocheted baby afghan you may already have. Or add a ring of matching flowers around the neck of a favorite stuffed toy.

The smiling feline, *right,* is more friendly than ferocious. The tiger's body parts are crocheted in rounds, then stuffed and stitched together; and his well-designed shaping makes him all the more huggable.

Because the yarn is acrylic and the stuffing is polyester, the toy is completely machine washable and dryable. An embroidered mouth, felt-circle eyes, and claws shaped with big stitches are the marks of his winning personality. Perky plaid bows add the finishing touch.

You can adapt this design to make other cats as well. For example, work the body in tan yarn and add a fringe mane around the face to create a king of the jungle. Or work the body in orange and glue on black felt dots to make a cheetah.

Crocheters who find a newborn in their midst will take a shine to the romper set, *opposite.* The two-piece outfit's generous size allows it to slip on easily over a tiny head, and crocheted ribbing keeps everything snugly in place.

This set is made of washable acrylic sport-weight yarn, and is a perfect choice for outfits for newborns.

Although pale pink and blue remain the hands-down favorites, consider the wide range of colors of yarn available in weights suitable for baby garments. For example, you might want to make an infant's outfit in white with touches of bright red or blue, instead of the traditional pastels.

Few animal toys come as well dressed as the trio at right. The knitted bear, cat, and bunny sport such grown-up clothes as a Fair Isle sweater and a cabled pullover.

The animals' heads, torsos, and legs are knitted in one piece, with color changes forming the separate body parts and clothing. The arms, ears, and the cat's skirt are worked separately and stitched onto the body.

Selecting materials for toys and clothing for newborns and infants requires special consideration.

Acrylic yarns are the most popular choices for baby garments because they withstand repeated machine washing and drying. Wool or wool-blend yarns need special treatment, and can cause minor irritation to sensitive skin.

When making crib toys or adding decorations to garments, avoid using buttons, beads, or trims that a baby could easily swallow. For dolls, substitute embroidered features or glued-on felt shapes.

Snugly and cozy, the crocheted baby afghan, *above*, adapts motifs from old-fashioned cross-stitch samplers. The 25 squares are made with sport-weight yarn in afghan stitches—a type of crochet that forms rows of uniformly shaped stitches.

Once the squares are crocheted, work the heart patterns, the letters, and the borders in cross-stitches with yarn and a tapestry needle. Then work the lacy edging along the outside border.

For a larger afghan, make 10 more squares, five with hearts and five with the numerals from one to 10.

KNIT AND CROCHET

Blanket, Cardigan, Cap, and Booties

Shown on pages 30–31.

Directions are for Size 6 Months. Changes for Sizes 1 Year and 18 Months follow in parentheses. Finished chest size is 19 (20, 21) inches. Blanket is 42x36 inches, including the border.

MATERIALS
Coats & Clark Red Heart Baby
  Yarn: 17 (18, 18) ounces of
  No. 680 green for complete
  set; 4 ounces to complete
  cardigan, cap, and booties
Size 5 knitting needles
Size D aluminum crochet hook
Five ½-inch-diameter buttons

Abbreviations: See page 47.
Gauge: Stockinette stitch: 6 sts = 1 inch; 8 rows = 1 inch

For the blanket
Starting at long edge, cast on 251 sts.
Rows 1–4: Knit.
Row 5: K 5, p 1, * (k 1, yo) 4 times; k 1, p 3, k 1, (k 2 tog) twice; (yo, k 1) 3 times; yo, (sl 1, k 1, psso) twice; k 3, p 3. Rep from * to last 11 sts, (k 1, yo) 4 times; k 1, p 1, k 5.
Row 6: K 6, * p 2, (p 2 tog) twice; p 3, k 3, p 15, k 3. Rep from * to last 15 sts, p 2, (p 2 tog) twice; p 3, k 6.
Row 7: K 5, p 1, * k 1, p 1, k 3 tog, p 1, k 1, p 3, (k 2 tog) twice; yo, k 1, yo, k 3, yo, k 1, yo, (sl 1, k 1, psso) twice; k 2, p 3. Rep from * to last 13 sts, k 1, p 1, k 3 tog, p 1, k 1, p 1, k 5.
Row 8: K 6, * p 5, k 3, p 15, k 3. Rep from * to last 11 sts, p 5, k 6.
Row 9: K 5, p 1, * (k 1, yo) 4 times; k 1, p 3, k 3, (k 2 tog) twice; (yo, k 1) 3 times; yo, (sl 1, k 1, psso) twice; k 1, p 3. Rep from * to last 11 sts, (k 1, yo) 4 times; k 1, p 1, k 5.
Row 10: K 6, * p 2, (p 2 tog) twice; p 3, k 3, p 15, k 3. Rep from * to last 15 sts, p 2, (p 2 tog) twice; p 3, k 6.
Row 11: K 5, p 1, * k 1, p 1, k 3 tog, p 1, k 1, p 3, k 2, (k 2 tog) twice; yo, k 1, yo, k 3, yo, k 1, yo, (sl 1, k 1, psso) twice; p 3. Rep from * to last 13 sts, k 1, p 1, k 3 tog, p 1, k 1, p 1, k 5.
Row 12: K 6, * p 5, k 3, p 15, k 3. Rep from * to last 11 sts, p 5, k 6. Rep Rows 5–12 until total length is 35½ inches, end with Row 8 of pat. Rep Rows 1–4 once. Bind off.

For the cardigan
Note: Cardigan is worked in one piece to underarm.

BODY: Starting at lower edge, cast on 129 (137, 145) sts.
Rows 1–3: Knit.
Row 4: K 5 and place these sts on safety pin for button band; k to last 5 sts and place these sts on another pin for buttonhole band.
Row 5: P 1, * (k 1, yo) 4 times; k 1, p 4 (5, 6), k 1, (k 2 tog) twice; (yo, k 1) 3 times; yo, (sl 1, k 1, psso) twice; k 3, p 4 (5, 6). Rep from * to last 6 sts, (k 1, yo) 4 times; k 1, p 1.
Row 6: K 1, * p 2, (p 2 tog) twice; p 3, k 4 (5, 6), p 15, k 4 (5, 6). Rep from * to last 10 sts, p 2, (p 2 tog) twice; p 3, k 1.
Row 7: P 1, * k 1, p 1, k 3 tog, p 1, k 1, p 4 (5, 6); (k 2 tog) twice; yo, k 1, yo, k 3, yo, k 1, yo, (sl 1, k 1, psso) twice; k 2, p 4 (5, 6). Rep from * to last 8 sts, k 1, p 1, k 3 tog, p 1, k 1, p 1.
Row 8: K 1, * p 5, k 4 (5, 6), p 15, k 4 (5, 6). Rep from * to last 6 sts, p 5, k 1.
Row 9: P 1, * (k 1, yo) 4 times; k 1, p 4 (5, 6), k 3, (k 2 tog) twice; (yo, k 1) 3 times; yo, (sl 1, k 1, psso) twice; k 1, p 4 (5, 6). Rep from * to last 6 sts, (k 1, yo) 4 times; k 1, p 1.
Row 10: K 1, * p 2, (p 2 tog) twice; p 3, k 4 (5, 6), p 15, k 4 (5,6). Rep from * to last 10 sts, p 2, (p 2 tog) twice; p 3, k 1.
Row 11: P 1, * k 1, p 1, k 3 tog, p 1, k 1, p 4 (5, 6), k 2, (k 2 tog) twice; yo, k 1, yo, k 3, yo, k 1, yo, (sl 1, k 1, psso) twice; p 4 (5, 6). Rep from * to last 8 sts, k 1, p 1, k 3 tog, p 1, k 1, p 1.
Row 12: K 1, * p 5, k 4 (5, 6), p 15, k 4 (5, 6). Rep from * to last 6 sts, p 5, k 1. Rep Rows 5–12 until total length is 5½ (6, 6¾) inches, end with Row 12 (8, 12).

Divide sts for upper sections as follows:
Dividing row (right side): K first 29 (32, 34) sts and place on stitch holder for Upper Right Front; k next 61 (63, 67) sts and place on another holder for Back. Leave remaining 29 (32, 34) sts on needle for Upper Left Front.

UPPER LEFT FRONT: Work in garter stitch (k each row) until length from dividing row is 3 (3¼, 3½) inches, end at front edge.

NECK AND SHOULDER SHAPING, *Row 1:* Bind off first 8 (8, 10) sts, work across.
Row 2: Work to last 2 sts, knit last 2 sts tog.
Row 3: Knit first 2 sts tog, work across.
Row 4: Rep Row 2.
For 1 Year and 18 Months sizes only: Rep Row 3. *For 6 Months size only:* Work 1 row even.
For all sizes: There are 18 (19, 20) sts on needle.
Next row: Bind off first 9 (9, 10) sts, work across.
Following row: Work even.
Bind off rem sts.

UPPER BACK: Slip the 61 (63, 67) sts from back holder onto needle. With wrong side facing, join yarn to first st. Work in garter stitch until length from dividing row is 4 (4¼, 4½) inches, end with a row worked on wrong side.

NECK AND SHOULDER SHAPING, *Rows 1-2:* Bind off 9 (9, 10) sts, k across.
Rows 3-4: Bind off 9 (10, 10) sts, k across. Bind off rem sts.

UPPER RIGHT FRONT: Sl 29 (32, 34) sts from right front holder to needle. Wrong side facing, join yarn to first st. Work as for Upper Left Front Section.

BUTTON BAND: Sl 5 button-band sts to needle, join yarn at inner edge. Work band in garter stitch until same length as front edge; bind off. With pins, mark position for 5 buttons on band having first pin ¾ inch from lower edge and last pin ¼ inch below neck edge.

BUTTONHOLE BAND: Sl the 5 sts from safety pin onto needle. With right side facing, join yarn to first st. Work in garter stitch up to line with first pin on button band, end at front edge.

First buttonhole row: K 1, k 2 tog, yo, k 2.

Second buttonhole row: K 5.

Work in garter stitch and make a buttonhole opposite each pin until length of band is same as opposite side. Bind off. Stitch bands to sweater edges. Sew on buttons; finish buttonholes.

SLEEVES: Starting at the lower edge, cast on 49 (53, 57) sts.

Rows 1–4: Knit.

Row 5 (right side): K 9, (10, 11), (yo, k 1) 4 times; p 4 (5, 6), k 1, (k 2 tog) twice; (yo, k 1) 3 times; yo, (sl 1, k 1, psso) twice; k 3, p 4 (5, 6), (k 1, yo) 4 times; k 9 (10, 11).

Row 6: K 8 (9, 10), p 2, (p 2 tog) twice; p 3, k 4 (5, 6), p 15, k 4 (5, 6), p 2, (p 2 tog) twice; p 3, k 8 (9, 10).

Row 7: K 9 (10, 11), p 1, k 3 tog, p 1, k 1, p 4 (5, 6), (k 2 tog) twice; yo, k 1, yo, k 3, yo, k 1, yo, (sl 1, k 1, psso) twice; k 2, p 4 (5, 6), k 1, p 1, k 3 tog, p 1, k 9 (10, 11).

Row 8: K 8 (9, 10), p 5, k 4 (5, 6), p 15, k 4 (5, 6), p 5, k 8 (9, 10).

Row 9: K 9 (10, 11), (yo, k 1) 4 times; p 4 (5, 6), k 3, (k 2 tog) twice; (yo, k 1) 3 times; yo, (sl 1, k 1, psso) twice; k 1, p 4 (5, 6), (k 1, yo) 4 times; k 9 (10, 11).

Row 10: K 8 (9, 10), p 2 (p 2 tog) twice; p 3, k 4 (5, 6), p 15, k 4 (5, 6), p 2, (p 2 tog) twice; p 3, k 8 (9, 10).

Row 11: K 9 (10, 11), p 1, k 3 tog, p 1, k 1, p 4 (5, 6), k 2, (k 2 tog) twice; yo, k 1, yo, k 3, yo, k 1, yo, (sl 1, k 1, psso) twice; p 4 (5, 6), k 1, p 1, k 3 tog, p 1, k 9 (10, 11).

Row 12: K 8 (9, 10), p 5, k 4 (5, 6), p 15, k 4 (5, 6), p 5, k 8 (9, 10). Rep Rows 5–12 for pat until total length is 6½ (7½, 8½) inches, end with Row 12. Work in garter stitch for 6 rows. Bind off.

Sew shoulder and sleeve seams. Sew in sleeves.

COLLAR: Right side facing, join yarn to third st in from right front corner. Pick up and k 97 sts evenly along neck edge to within last 2 sts from left front corner.

Row 1: K 5, p 2, * (k 1, yo) 4 times; k 1, p 3, k 1, (k 2 tog) twice; (yo, k 1) 3 times; yo, (sl 1, k 1, psso) twice; k 3, p 3. Rep from * to last 12 sts, (k 1, yo) 4 times; k 1, p 2, k 5.

Row 2: K 7, * p 2, (p 2 tog) twice; p 3, k 3, p 15, k 3. Rep from * to last 16 sts, p 2, (p 2 tog) twice; p 3, k 7.

Row 3: K 5, p 2, * k 1, p 1, k 3 tog, p 1, k 1, p 3, (k 2 tog) twice; yo, k 1, yo, k 3, yo, k 1, yo, (sl 1, k 1, psso) twice; k 2, p 3. Rep from * to last 14 sts, k 1, p 1, k 3 tog, p 1, k 1, p 2, k 5.

Row 4: K 7, * p 5, k 3, p 15, k 3. Rep from * to last 12 sts, p 5, k 7.

Row 5: K 5, p 2, * (k 1, yo) 4 times; k 1, p 3, k 3, (k 2 tog) twice; (yo, k 1) 3 times; yo, (sl 1, k 1, psso) twice; k 1, p 3. Rep from * to last 12 sts, (k 1, yo) 4 times; k 1, p 2, k 5.

Row 6: K 7, * p 2, (p 2 tog) twice; p 3, k 3, p 15, k 3. Rep from * to last 16 sts, p 2, (p 2 tog) twice; p 3, k 7.

Row 7: K 5, p 2, * k 1, p 1, k 3 tog, p 1, k 1, p 3, k 2, (k 2 tog) twice; yo, k 1, yo, k 3, yo, k 1, yo, (sl 1, k 1, psso) twice; p 3. Rep from * to last 14 sts, k 1, p 1, k 3 tog, p 1, k 1, p 2, k 5.

Row 8: K 7, * p 5, k 3, p 15, k 3. Rep from * to last 12 sts; ending p 5, k 7. Rep last 8 rows once more. Bind off.

TIE (make 2): With crochet hook and 2 strands of yarn, make chain 13 inches long. Fasten off. Knot each end and draw tie through Row 5 of each sleeve.

For the cap

Starting at lower edge, cast on 86 sts.

Rows 1–3: Knit.

Row 4 (right side): * K 3, p 3, (k 1, yo) 4 times; k 1, p 3, k 1, (k 2 tog) twice; (yo, k 1) 3 times; yo, (sl 1, k 1, psso) twice; k 3, p 3, (k 1, yo) 4 times; k 1, p 3, k 3. Rep from * once.

Row 5: * K 6, p 2, (p 2 tog) twice; p 3, k 3, p 15, k 3, p 2, (p 2 tog) twice; p 3, k 6. Rep from * once.

Row 6: * K 3, p 3, k 1, p 1, k 3 tog, p 1, k 1, p 3, (k 2 tog) twice; yo, k 1, yo, k 3, yo, k 1, yo, (sl 1, k 1, psso) twice; k 2, p 3, k 1, p 1, k 3 tog, p 1, k 1, p 3, k 3. Rep from * once.

Row 7: * K 6, p 5, k 3, p 15, k 3, p 5, k 6. Rep from * once.

Row 8: * K 3, p 3, (k 1, yo) 4 times; k 1, p 3, k 3, (k 2 tog) twice; (yo, k 1) 3 times; yo, (sl 1, k 1, psso) twice; k 1, p 3, (k 1, yo) 4 times; k 1, p 3, k 3. Rep from * once.

Row 9: * K 6, p 2, (p 2 tog) twice; p 3, k 3, p 15, k 3, p 2, (p 2 tog) twice; p 3, k 6. Rep from * once.

Row 10: * K 3, p 3, k 1, p 1, k 3 tog, p 1, k 1, p 3, k 2, (k 2 tog) twice; yo, k 1, yo, k 3, yo, k 1, yo, (sl 1, k 1, psso) twice; p 3, k 1, p 1, k 3 tog, p 1, k 1, p 3, k 3. Rep from * once.

Row 11: * K 6, p 5, k 3, p 15, k 3, p 5, k 6. Rep from * once.

Rows 12–9: Rep Rows 4–11.

Row 20: * K 3, place marker on needle, p 3, (k 1, yo) 4 times; k 1, p 3, k 1, (k 2 tog) twice; (yo, k 1) 3 times; yo, (sl 1, k 1, psso) twice; k 3, p 3, (k 1, yo) 4 times; k 1, p 3, place marker on needle, k 3. Rep from * once—4 markers on needle. *Always slip markers on every row.*

Row 21: Work as for Row 5.

Rows 22–24: Continuing to work in pat, dec one st before first marker, following second marker, before third marker, and following fourth marker on next and every other row once.

Row 25: Work even.

Row 26: Work to second marker, dec one st, complete row.

Row 27: Removing markers, work across.

CROWN SHAPING: Dec 12 sts evenly spaced on next row and every other row, work in garter stitch for 5 rows. K one row. Draw a double strand of yarn through sts on needle. Draw sts together and secure. Join the 2 back edges together and sew to neck edge.

EAR FLAP (make 2): Cast on 14 sts. Work in garter stitch for 8 rows.

continued

Next row: K 1, k 2 sts tog, k to last 3 sts, k 2 sts tog, k 1. Rep last row until 4 sts remain.

STRAP: Work even over 4 sts in garter stitch for 9 inches. Bind off. Sew flaps in place. Make pompom and attach to crown of cap.

For the booties

Starting at center of sole, cast on 37 sts.

Row 1 and all odd-numbered rows: Knit.

Row 2: Inc 1 st in first st, k 16, inc 1 st in each of next 2 sts, k 16, inc 1 st in next st, k 1—41 sts.

Row 4: Inc in first st, k 18, inc in each of next 2 sts, k 18, inc in next st, k 1—45 sts.

Row 6: Inc in first st, k 20, inc one st in each of next 2 sts, k 20, inc in next st, k 1—49 sts.

Row 8: Inc in first st, k 22, inc one st in each of next 2 sts, k 22, inc in next st, k 1—53 sts. Mark last row worked for wrong side. Work in garter stitch for 8 rows.

TO SHAPE INSTEP, *Row 1:* K 31, sl 1, k 1, psso, do not work over remaining sts. Turn.

Row 2: K 10, k 2 tog. Turn.

Row 3: K 10, sl 1, k 1, psso. Turn. *Rows 4–15:* Rep Rows 2 and 3 alternately.

Row 16: K 10, k 2 tog, k 13.

Row 17: K 37.

BOOTIE EDGING, *Row 1—Eyelet row:* K 2, * (yo, k 2 tog) 8 times; k 2. Rep from * across, end with k 1. *Rows 2–3:* Knit.

Row 4: K 12, (k 2 tog) twice; (yo, k 1) 3 times; yo, (sl 1, k 1, psso) twice; k 14.

Row 5 and all odd-numbered rows: K 11, p 15, k 11.

Row 6: K 11, (k 2 tog) twice; yo, k 1, yo, k 3, yo, k 1, yo, (sl 1, k 1, psso) twice; k 13.

Row 8: K 14, (k 2 tog) twice; (yo, k 1) 3 times; yo, (sl 1, k 1, psso) twice; k 12.

Row 10: K 13, (k 2 tog) twice; yo, k 1, yo, k 3, yo, k 1, yo, (sl 1, k 1, psso) twice; k 11.

Rows 12–20: Rep Rows 4–12.

Rows 21–24: Knit. Bind off. Sew back and sole seams.

TIE: With two strands of yarn held together and crochet hook, make a chain 18 inches long. Fasten off. Knot each end and draw tie through eyelet row.

Infant's Dress with Eyelet Bodice

Shown on page 32.

Directions are for Size 6 Months. Changes for sizes 12 and 18 Months follow in parentheses. Finished chest size is 19 (20, 21) inches.

MATERIALS

Coats & Clark Red Heart Luster Sheen: 5 (6, 6) ounces of No. 024 Soft Lullaby
Size four 24-inch circular knitting needle
Size 4 straight needles
Size 0 steel crochet hook
Stitch holders; 4 small buttons

Abbreviations: See page 47.
Gauge: 6 sts = 1 inch; 8 rows = 1 inch.

INSTRUCTIONS

SKIRT (work in rnds): Beg at lower edge with circular needle, cast on 160 (176, 192) sts. Place marker on needle to indicate end of rnd. Slip marker on every rnd; join.

Rnd 1: Knit. *Rnd 2:* Purl.

Rnds 3–4: Rep Rnds 1 and 2.

Work in st st (knit every rnd) until total length is 6¼ (6¾, 7¼) inches.

Next rnd: * K 2, k 2 tog; rep from * around—120 (132, 144) sts. Rep Rnds 1-4 once.

Knit next 2 rnds.

Next rnd—Eyelet rnd: * K 2, yo, k 2 tog; rep from * around—120 (132, 144) sts.

Rep Rnds 1–4 once. Remove marker and divide sts as follows: With straight needle, bind off first 3 (4, 4) sts; k across 57 (62, 68) sts. Place rem sts on holder for front.

LEFT BACK ARMHOLE SHAPING: With straight needles, work in rows in st st, (k on right side of work, p on wrong side of work). Bind off 3 (4, 4) sts; p across until 27 (29, 32) sts on needle; place remaining sts on another holder for right back section.

Following row: K across to last 2 sts, k 2 tog.

Next row: Purl. Rep last 2 rows 2 (2, 3) times more. Work even in st st until length from beg of armhole measures 3½ (3¾, 4) inches, end with k row.

SHOULDER SHAPING, *Row 1:* Bind off first 7 sts, p across.

Row 2: Knit.

Row 3: Bind off 7 (8, 8) sts, p across. Slip remaining 10 (11, 13) sts on another holder for back of neck.

RIGHT BACK ARMHOLE SHAPING: Slip 27 (29, 32) sts from holder onto needle with wrong side facing.

Row 1: P across.

Row 2: K 2 tog, k across.

Row 3: P. Rep last 2 rows alternately 2 (2, 3) times. Work even in st st until length is same as on left back armhole; end with p row.

SHOULDER SHAPING, *Row 1:* Bind off 7 sts; k across.

Row 2: P across.

Row 3: Bind off 7 (8, 8) sts; k across.

Row 4: Rep Row 2. Slip remaining 10 (11, 13) sts on another holder for back of neck.

FRONT ARMHOLE SHAPINGS: With right side facing, slip the 60 (66, 72) sts from holder onto the needle.

Rows 1–2: Bind off 3 (4, 4) sts, complete row.

Row 3: K 2 tog, work across to last 2 sts, k 2 tog.

Row 4: Purl.

Row 5: K 2 tog, k 9 (11, 14); (yo, k 2 tog, k 12) twice; yo, k 2 tog, k 9 (11, 14), k 2 tog.

Row 6: Purl. Rep Rows 3 and 4 1 (1, 2) more times. Work next 2 (2, 0) rows even.

Following row: K 2 (4, 6); (yo, k 2 tog, k 12) 3 times; k 2 (4, 6).

Next 5 rows: Work even.

Following row: K 9 (11, 13); (yo, k 2 tog, k 12) twice; yo, k 2 tog; k 9 (11, 13).

Next row: Purl.

LEFT NECK AND SHOULDER SHAPING, *Row 1:* K 20 (21, 22); place remaining sts on a holder. Decreasing one st at neck edge on every row, work until there are 14 (15, 15) sts on needle. Work even until length from beg of armhole shaping is 3½ (3¾, 4) inches, end at armhole edge.

Next row: Bind off 7 sts, complete row.

Following row: Work even. Bind off.

RIGHT NECK, SHOULDER SHAPING: Leave center 8 (10, 12) sts on holder for center front; place remaining sts from holder onto needle. Join yarn at neck edge and k across—20 (21, 22) sts. Complete as for other side.

SLEEVES: Starting at lower edge with straight needles cast on 34 (36, 40) sts.

Rows 1-2: Knit.

Row 3: K 4 (3, 4); * k in front and in back of next st—inc made; rep from * to last 4 (3, 4) sts; k last 4 (3, 4) sts—60 (66, 72) rem.

Row 4: Purl. *Row 5:* Knit. Work even in st st for 3 (5, 7) rows.

Next row: K 8 (11, 14); (yo, k 2 tog, k 12) 3 times; yo, k 2 tog; k 8 (11, 14). Work 3 (5, 5) rows even.

TOP SHAPING, *Rows 1-2:* Bind off 3 (4, 4) sts, complete row.

Row 3: K 3 tog—2-st dec made; k 9 (11, 14); (yo, k 2 tog, k 12) twice; yo, k 2 tog; k 9 (11, 14); k 3 tog. *Row 4:* Purl.

Row 5: Dec 2 sts at beg and end of row, k across. *Row 6:* Purl. *Rows 7-10:* Rep last 2 rows twice.

Row 11: K 3 tog, k 8 (10, 13); yo, k 2 tog, k 12, yo, k 2 tog; k 8 (10, 13); k 3 tog. *Row 12:* Purl.

Continue to work in st st, dec 2 sts at each end on next row and every other row until there are 18 (18, 16) sts on needle.

Next row: Purl. Bind off. Sew shoulder seams.

NECKBAND, *Row 1:* Right side facing and joining yarn at left back neck edge, k 10 (11, 13) sts from holder; pick up and k 10 (14, 16) sts along left front neck edge; k 8 (10, 12) sts from front holder; pick up and k 10 (14, 16) sts along right front neck edge; k 10 (11, 13) sts from right back holder—48 (60, 70) sts.

Rows 2-4: Knit. Bind off.

NECKBAND FINISHING: With crochet hook, join yarn at upper right back corner of neck edge, ch 1, sc in same place; sc evenly around back opening to upper left back corner; ch 1, turn. With pins, mark position for 4 buttonholes along the left back edge. Work along left edge only as follows: * sc in each sc to next pin; ch 3, skip next 2 sc, sc in next sc—buttonhole made. Rep from * until all buttonholes have been completed, sc in each sc to center of back opening; ch 1, turn.

Next row: Sc in each sc across to neck opening, making 3 sc in each ch-3 loop. Fasten off. Sew on buttons.

Sew sleeve seams; sew sleeves to dress, easing to fit.

TWISTED CORD: Cut four 3-yard lengths of yarn; knot together at one end. Place knotted end over doorknob or hook, twist other end in one direction until yarn is taut. Holding yarn, fold in half and release folded end a little at a time to make cord. Lace cord through eyelet holes on waist of dress, trim to length desired, and knot ends to secure.

Beribboned Afghan

Shown on page 33.

Finished size is 33x33 inches.

MATERIALS
Coats & Clark sport-weight yarn: 11 ounces of No. 3 off-white
Scraps of sport-weight yarns in pastel colors
Size F aluminum crochet hook
Size 1 steel crochet hook
10½ yards each of ⅜-inch-wide green and pink ribbon

Abbreviations: See page 47.
Gauge: 5 pat sts = 1 inch; 4 pat rows = 1 inch.

INSTRUCTIONS
MOTIF (make 25): With Size F hook, ch 26.

Row 1: Sc in second ch from hook, * dc in next ch, sc in following ch; rep from * across—25 sts. Mark this row for right side of work. Ch 3, turn. Hereafter ch-3 always counts as 1 dc.

Row 2: * Sc in next dc, dc in following sc; rep from * across—25 sts. Ch 1, turn.

Row 3: Sc in first dc, * dc in next sc, sc in following dc; rep from * across, end with sc in top of ch-3. Ch 3, turn.

Rows 4-19: Rep Rows 2 and 3 alternately; at end of Row 19, ch 5, turn.

Make border as follows: Rnd 1: Working across sts on last row, * skip ½ inch along edge of Motif, (dc in next st, ch 2, skip about ½ inch along edge) 9 times; in next corner st make dc, ch 3 and dc—corner made; ch 2. Rep from * 2 times; * skip about ½ inch along edge, (dc in next st, ch 2, skip about ½ inch) 9 times; in last corner st make dc, ch 3. Join with sl st to third ch of ch-5 to complete last corner. Fasten off.

ASSEMBLY OF MOTIFS: Right side facing and working in *back* loops only, whipstitch motifs together. Make 5 strips of 5 motifs each; join strips.

OUTSIDE EDGING: With right side facing, join yarn in any corner sp. Ch 6, dc in same sp—starting corner sp made; * ch 1, dc in next dc, (ch 2, dc in next dc) 10 times; ch 1, dc in joining between motifs. Rep from * to next corner sp, ** in corner sp make dc, ch 3 and dc, *** ch 1, dc in next dc, (ch 2, dc in next dc) 10 times; ch 1, dc in joining between motifs. Rep from *** to next corner. Rep from ** around. Join to third ch of ch-6. Fasten off.

continued

RIBBON TRIM: Using photograph, page 33, as a guide, weave pink and green ribbons across strips. Begin weaving from underside for both colors so ribbons lie parallel to each other. Weave ribbons around the outside edges last. Cut ribbons at corners and begin a new strip. When ribbons are all woven, adjust so afghan lies flat and even. Fold back raw edges of ribbons and sew in place.

For the flowers

Make 20. With Size 1 hook, ch 5, join with sl st to make ring. (Ch 3, 2 trc in ring, ch 3, sl st in ring) 5 times—5 petals. Fasten off.

For the leaves

Make 20. With Size 1 hook, ch 7, sl st in second ch from hook, sc in next ch, 2 dc in next ch, 2 trc in next ch, dc and sc in next ch; sl st in last ch. Working in opposite side of ch, work sc in next ch, 2 dc in each of next 2 ch, sc in next ch; sl st in next ch. Fasten off.

Tack a leaf and flower together and attach to afghan with French knots at all intersections except one. Make one grouping of five flowers and three leaves and sew at remaining intersection.

Baby Tiger Toy

Shown on page 34.

Tiger is about 11½ inches tall.

MATERIALS

Coats & Clark Red Heart 4-Ply Yarn: 2 skeins No. 261 maize; 1 skein No. 1 white
J & P Coats Deluxe Six-Strand Floss: 1 skein each of No. 122 pink and No. 12 black
Size J aluminum crochet hook
Small pieces of black and blue felt for eyes and nose
½ yard of 1¼-inch-wide ribbon
Polyester stuffing

Abbreviations: See page 47.
Gauge: 4 stitches = 1 inch; 4 rounds = 1 inch

INSTRUCTIONS

HEAD: Beg at center front, with white, ch 4. Join with sl st to form ring.

Rnd 1: Ch 1, make 6 sc in ring. Do not join rnds; mark last st of rnd with safety pin and move with each succeeding rnd to indicate beg of each rnd.

Rnd 2: Work 2 sc in each sc—12 sc. *Rnd 3:* (Sc in next sc; 2 sc in next sc) 6 times—18 sc.

Rnd 4: (Sc in next 2 sc, 2 sc in next sc) 6 times—24 sc.

Rnd 5: (Sc in next 2 sc, 2 sc in next sc) 8 times—32 sc.

Rnd 6: (Sc in next 4 sc, 2 sc in next sc) 6 times; sc in last 2 sc—38 sc.

Rnds 7–9: Sc in each sc around; on last st of Rnd 9, make color change as follows: draw up lp in last st, drop white, yo with maize and draw through 2 lps on hook.

Rnd 10: With maize, work even.

Rnd 11: Sc in next 10 sc, (inc in next sc, sc in next sc) 9 times; inc in next sc—increases will form forehead; sc in next 9 sc—48 sc.

Rnd 12: Sc in next 10 sc, (inc in next sc, sc in next 2 sc) 9 times; inc in next sc, sc in next 10 sc—58 sc. *Rnds 13-22:* Work even.

Rnd 23: * Sc in next 2 sc; *draw up a lp in each of next 2 sc, yarn over and draw through all lps on hook—dec made.* Rep from * to last 2 sc, sc in last 2 sc—44 sc.

Rnd 24: * Dec over next 2 sc, sc in next 2 sc; rep from * around.

Rnd 25: * Sc in next 2 sc, dec over next 2 sc; rep from * to last sc, sc in last sc—25 sc.

Rnd 26: * Sc in next sc, dec over next 2 sc; rep from * to last sc, sc in last sc—17 sc.

Rnd 27: * Dec over next 2 sc, sc in next sc; rep from * to last 2 sc, dec over last 2 sc—11sc. Fasten off; leave a 10-inch end. Stuff head; draw yarn end through sts of last rnd and pull together; secure end.

EARS (make 2): With maize, ch 6. *Row 1:* Sc in second ch from hook and in next 3 ch; 3 sc in last ch. Working along opposite side of chain, sc in next 4 ch; do not join. Ch 1, turn.

Row 2: Sc in next 5 sc, 3 sc in next sc, sc in next 5 sc; ch 1, turn.

Row 3: Sc in next 5 sc, 2 sc in next sc, sc in next sc, 2 sc in next sc, sc in next 5 sc; ch 1, turn.

Row 4: Sc in next 6 sc, 2 sc in next sc, sc in next sc, 2 sc in next sc, sc in next 6 sc; ch 1, turn.

Row 5: Sc in next 6 sc, (2 sc in next sc, sc in next sc) twice; 2 sc in next sc, sc in next 6 sc—20 sc. Fasten off; leave 10-inch end for sewing. Slightly gather straight edge and sew ears in place on head, using photograph, page 34, as a guide.

BODY: Beg at neck with maize, ch 4. Join with sl st to form ring.

Rnds 1–4: Work as for Rnds 1-4 of Head—24 sc on last rnd.

Rows 5–6: Work even. *Rnd 7:* * Sc in next 3 sc, 2 sc in next sc; rep from * around—30 sc.

Rnd 8: * Sc in next 4 sc, 2 sc in next sc; rep from * around—36 sc. *Rnd 9:* Work even.

Rnd 10: (2 sc in next sc, sc in next 8 sc) 4 times— 40 sts.

Rnd 11: Sc in next 3 sc, (2 sc in next sc, sc in next 9 sc) 3 times; 2 sc in next sc, sc in last 6 sc—44 sc. *Rnds 12–19:* Work even.

Rnd 20: (Sc in next 10 sc, inc in next sc) 4 times—48 sc.

Rnds 21–30: Work even.

Rnds 31–32: * Sc in next 2 sc, dec over next 2 sc; rep from * around—27 sc on last rnd.

Rnds 33–34: * Sc in next sc, dec in next 2 sc; rep from * around—12 sc on last rnd. Finish as for Head. Sew head to body at neck edge.

HIND LEGS (make 2): Using maize, ch 4; join to form ring.

Rnds 1–4: Work as for Head—24 sc. *Rnd 5:* (Sc in next 5 sc, inc in next sc) 4 times—28 sc.

Rnds 6–9: Work even.

Rnd 10: Sc in next 9 sc; (dec over next 2 sc) 5 times; sc in next 9 sc—23 sc.

Rnds 11–16: Work even; fasten off leaving a 10-inch end. Stuff leg and sew in place at base of body.

FRONT LEGS (make 2): With maize, ch 4; join to form ring.

Rnds 1–4: Work as for Head—24 sc.

Rnd 5: Sc in next 8 sc, 2 sc in next sc, sc in next 11 sc, 2 sc in next sc, sc in last 3 sc—26 sc.

Rnds 6–7: Work even.

Rnd 8: Sc in next 8 sc, (dec over next 2 sc) 5 times; sc in next 8 sc—21 sc.

Rnds 9–14: Work even; fasten off, leaving a 10-inch end. Stuff leg and sew in place.

TAIL: With maize, ch 4; join with sl st to form ring.

Rnd 1: Ch 1, make 5 sc in ring. Do not join rnds; mark last st of each rnd to indicate beg of each rnd. *Rnd 2:* Sc in each sc—5 sc.

Rnd 3: Inc in next sc, sc in each sc around—6 sc.

Rnds 4–6: Work even.

Rnds 7–18: Rep Rnds 3-6 three times.

Rnds 19–28: Work even over 9 sc. Fasten off; leave a 10-inch end. Stuff tail and sew in place at base of body.

FINISHING: Cut two ⅞-inch-diameter circles of blue felt and two ½-inch-diameter circles of black felt; glue black pieces atop blue pieces for eyes. Cut a 1-inch-diameter piece of black felt for nose; trim to shape. Glue eyes and nose in place. With black floss, embroider a curved line of back stitches between Rnds 6 and 7 for mouth. Make whiskers with three strands of black floss and sew to face. With 6 strands of pink floss, stitch top edge on all legs by drawing a strand over Rnds 4–7 and pulling in slightly to form toes. Add ribbon bow to neck.

Crocheted Sweater and Shorts

Shown on page 35.

Directions are for Size 6 Months. Changes for Sizes 1 Year and 18 Months are in parentheses. Finished chest size is 19 (20, 21) inches.

MATERIALS
Coats & Clark Red Heart sport-yarn: 3 (3, 4) ounces of No. 1 white and 2 (3, 3) ounces of No. 681 mist green
Sizes F and I aluminum crochet hooks
Four ⅜-inch-diameter buttons
½ yard of waistband elastic

Abbreviations: See page 47.
Gauge: With Size I hook; 9 sts (including ch-1 sps) = 2 inches; 8 rows = 2 inches

INSTRUCTIONS

For the sweater
BACK RIBBING: Beginning at narrow edge of ribbing, with F hook and white, ch 7.

Row 1: Sc in second ch from hook and in each ch across—6 sc. Ch 1, turn.

Row 2: Sc in *back* lp of each sc across, ch 1, turn. Rep Row 2 until ribbing (not stretched) is 10 (10½, 11) inches. At end of last row ch 1, *do not turn.*

BODY: Working on one long edge, make 45 (49, 53) sc evenly spaced across edge. Ch 1, turn.

Change to I hook and work in pat as follows:

Row 1: Sc in first sc; * ch 1, skip next sc, sc in next sc; rep from * across—45 (49, 53) sts counting each ch-1 sp as a st. Do not count turning-ch as a st. Ch 1, turn.

Row 2 (right side): Sc in first sc and in next ch-1 sp; * ch 1, sc in next ch-1 sp; rep from * to last sc. *Draw up a lp in last sc, drop white, with green, yo and draw through the 2 lps on hook—color change made.* Fasten off white. With green, ch 1, turn.

Row 3: Sc in first sc, * ch 1, sc in next ch-1 sp; rep from * to last 2 sc, ch 1, skip next sc, sc in last sc changing color to white. Fasten off green. Ch 1, turn.

Row 4: With white, sc in first sc and in next ch-1 sp; * ch 1, sc in next ch-1 sp; rep from * to last sc, sc in last sc. Ch 1, turn.

Row 5: Sc in first sc, * ch 1, sc in next ch-1 sp; rep from * to last 2 sc, ch 1, skip next sc, sc in last sc. Ch 1, turn.

Rows 6–7: Rep Rows 2 and 3. With white only, rep Rows 4 and 5 until total length is 6½ (7, 7½) inches, end with Row 4 on wrong side. Ch 1, turn.

ARMHOLE SHAPING, *Row 1:* Sl st in first 4 sts, ch 1, * sc in next ch-1 sp, ch 1; rep from * across to last 4 sts—37 (41, 45) sts. Ch 1, turn.

Rows 2–3: Rep Rows 2 and 3 of Back. With white only, rep Rows 4 and 5 of Back until length from first row of armhole shaping is 4 (4¼, 4½) inches, end with Row 4 on wrong side; fasten off. Mark the 9th (9th, 11th) st in from each end of last row to indicate end of shoulder seams.

FRONT: Work the same as for Back through Row 3 of Armhole Shaping.

Next row: Rep Row 4 of Back. Ch 1, turn.

LEFT NECK AND SHOULDER SHAPING, *Row 1:* Sc in first sc, (ch 1, sc in next ch-1 sp) 8 (9, 10) times; do not work over remaining sts. Ch 1, turn.

Rows 2–12: Rep Rows 4 and 5 of pat 5 times; rep Row 4 once.

Row 13: Sc in first sc, (ch 1, sc in next ch-1 sp) 5 (5, 6) times; do not work over remaining sts. Ch 1, turn.

Row 14: Rep Row 4.

Row 15: Sc in first sc, (ch 1, sc in next ch-1 sp) 4 (4, 5) times; do not work over remaining sts. Ch 1, turn. Rep Rows 4 and 5 until length is same as Back, end with Row 4. Fasten off.

RIGHT NECK AND SHOULDER SHAPING, *Row 1:* With right side of work facing, skip the next 3 sts after Row 1 of Left Neck and Shoulder Shaping (these 3 sts are at center front neck opening); join white in next ch-1 sp; ch 1, sc in same sp, (ch 1, sc in next ch-1 sp) 7 (8, 9) times; ch 1, skip next sc, sc in last sc.

Rows 2–12: Rep Rows 4 and 5 of stitch pat 5 times, then rep Row 4 once more.

continued

KNIT AND CROCHET

Row 13: Sl st in first 6 (8, 8) sts, ch 1, (sc in next ch-1 sp, ch 1) 5 (5, 6) times; sc in last sc. Ch 1, turn.

Row 14: Rep Row 4 of stitch pat.

Row 15: Sl st in first 2 sts, ch 1, (sc in next ch-1 sp, ch 1) 4 (4, 5) times; sc in last sc. Ch 1, turn. Rep Rows 4 and 5 of stitch pat until length is same as on Back, end with Row 4. Fasten off.

SLEEVE RIBBING: Work as for Ribbing on Back until ribbing (not stretched) is 4½ (4½, 4¾) inches. At end of last row ch 1, *do not turn.*

SLEEVES: Working across the long edge, make 23 (25, 29) sc evenly spaced. Ch 1, turn.

Change to I hook and work in pat as follows: *Rows 1–4:* Work as for Rows 1–4 of Back, changing to green at end of Row 4—23 (25, 29) sts. Ch 1, turn.

Row 5: With green, work as for Row 3 of Back changing to white at end of row. Ch 1, turn.

Row 6: With white, work as for Row 4 of Back. Ch 1, turn.

Row 7 (with white only): Rep Row 5 of pat. Ch 1, turn.

Row 8—inc row: Sc in first sc; *in next ch-1 sp make sc, ch 1 and sc—2-st inc made;* * ch 1, sc in next ch-1 sp. Rep from * to last sc; *ch 1, sc in same sp where last sc was made, sc in last sc—2-st inc made.* Ch 1, turn.

Rows 9–13: Rep Rows 5 and 4 of stitch pat twice then rep Row 5.

Rep last 6 rows (Rows 8–13) twice more—35 (37, 41) sts.

Next 2 (4, 6) rows: Rep Rows 4 and 5 of stitch pat alternately changing to green on the last row. Ch 1, turn.

Last row: With green, rep Row 4 of stitch pat. Fasten off. Sew shoulder seams.

NECK AND FRONT EDGING, *Row 1:* With *wrong* side of work facing and F hook, join green to end st at center front on Row 1 of Left Neck and Shoulder Shaping, ch 1, sc in joining; keeping work flat, sc evenly spaced along left

front opening to neck corner; 3 sc in corner, sc evenly around neck edge to right front corner; 3 sc in corner; sc evenly along right front edge of opening. Ch 1, turn.

Row 2: Sc in each sc around, making 3 sc in center sc at each corner. Fasten off.

BUTTON LOOPS: With straight pins, mark position for 4 button loops on left front edge of opening. Make a button loop on edge at each pin as follows: With F hook and green, join yarn to sc on edge, * ch 4, skip next sc on edge, sl st in next sc. Rep from * three times more. Fasten off.

FINISHING: Sew sleeve and side seams. Sew on buttons.

For the shorts

FRONT WAIST RIBBING: Beg at narrow edge of ribbing, with green and F hook, ch 9. Work as for Ribbing on Back over 8 sc until ribbing measures 8 (8½, 9) inches. At end of last row, ch 1, do not turn.

FRONT: Working across long edge, make 41 (45, 49) sc evenly spaced. Ch 1, turn.

Change to I hook. *Row 1:* Work as for Row 1 of sweater Back—41 (45, 49) sts. Ch 1, turn.

Rep Rows 4 and 5 of *stitch pat* of Back until total piece measures 3 inches, end with Row 5.

Next row: Rep Row 8 of Sleeves—45 (49, 53) sts. Ch 1, turn.

Rep Rows 5 and 4 of pat until total length is 6½ (7¼, 8) inches, end with Row 4. Ch 1, turn.

FIRST LEG SHAPING, *Row 1:* Sc in first sc, (ch 1, sc in next ch-1 sp) 9 (10, 11) times; do not work over remaining sts. Ch 1, turn.

Next 2 rows: Rep Rows 4 and 5 of pat. Fasten off.

SECOND LEG SHAPING, *Row 1:* Right side facing, skip next 7 sts after Row 1 of First Leg Shaping; join yarn in next ch-1 sp, ch 1, sc in same sp, ch 1, (sc in next ch-1 sp) 8 (9, 10) times; ch 1, skip next sc, sc in last sc. Ch 1, turn.

Next 2 rows: Rep Rows 4 and 5 of stitch pat. Fasten off.

BACK: Work same as FRONT.

LEG RIBBING (make 2): Starting at narrow edge of ribbing, with F hook, ch 6. Work as for Ribbing on Back over 5 sc until ribbing measures 4½ (5, 5) inches. Fasten off.

FINISHING: Sew side seams. Attach leg ribbings to each leg. Sew leg and crotch seam. Add elastic to waist. Sew on buttons.

Knitted Bear, Cat, and Bunny

Shown on page 36.

Animals are approximately 10 inches high, excluding ears.

MATERIALS
Brunswick Pomfret sport yarn: One (50-gram) ball each of No. 5681 chestnut heather, No. 5281 sea oats heather, No. 544 dartmouth green, No. 557 cranberry, No. 599 granite heather, No. 589 mauve heather, No. 5031 medium yellow, No. 563 cambridge heather, No. 560 black, and No. 500 white
Size 4 knitting needles
Two cable needles
Polyester fiberfill
Scraps of black, white, gold, pink, and red felt
Bits of black, gray, white, and pink embroidery floss
Carpet thread

Abbreviations: See page 47.
Gauge: 13 st = 2 inches; 8 rows = 1 inch

INSTRUCTIONS
Instructions for individual animals will follow. When a row is not indicated, work even in stockinette stitch. Knit odd-numbered rows and purl even-numbered rows. Rep instructions after * to complete a row.

For the bear

BEAR FRONT: Beg with head, using chestnut, cast on 16 sts.

Rows 1, 3 and 5: K, inc 1 st each side—22 sts end of Row 5.

Row 6-22: Work even in st st.

Row 23: Attach sea oats, k across.

Rows 24-26: Work ribbing k 1, p 1.

Rows 27-40: Work even in st st.

Rows 41-45: Work even following color chart for bear's sweater, *right.*

Row 46: With sea oats, p across.

Rows 47-49: Work ribbing k 1, p 1.

Row 50: Attach green, p across.

Rows 51-56: Work even in st st.

Row 57: K 11 sts; sl rem 11 sts to holder.

Rows 58-72: St st on 11 sts.

Rows 73-75: Work ribbing k 1, p 1.

Row 76: Attach chestnut, p across.

Rows 77-80: Work even in st st.

Rows 81 and 83: K, dec 1 st each side.

Rows 82 and 84: P across. Do not decrease.

Bind off rem 7 sts. Sl sts on holder to needle and work other leg to correspond.

BEAR BACK: Work as for front through Row 52.

BEAR TAIL, *Row 1:* Slip first 8 sts to holder. With chestnut, k 6. Put next 8 sts on holder.

Rows 2-4: Work even in st st.

Row 5: Dec 1 st each side.

Row 6: Work even.

Row 7: Inc 1 st each side.

Rows 8-11: Work even in st st. Return all sts to needle.

Row 53 of back: With green yarn, k across.

Complete back as for front.

ARMS (make 2): With sea oats, cast on 22 sts. Work even in st st for 12 rows.

Rows 13-17: Work from color chart for bear's sweater.

Row 18: With sea oats, p across.

Rows 19-21: Work ribbing k 1, p 1.

Row 22: With chestnut, p across.

Rows 23-25: Work even in st st.

Row 26: P 11 sts; sl rem 11 sts to holder.

Rows 27 and 29: Working on the 11 sts, k *and at same time* dec 1 st each side.

Rows 28-30: Work even. Bind off rem 7 sts. Work other side of paw to correspond.

EARS (make two): With chestnut, cast on 8 sts. Work 4 rows st st. *Rows 5 and 7:* Dec 1 st each side.

Rows 6, 8-10, and 12: Work even.

Rows 11 and 13: Inc 1 st each side.

Work even for 5 more rows. Bind off.

FINISHING: Fold each arm in half and sew seams. Stuff lightly. Fold each ear in half and sew seams. Sew seams of tail.

Beginning with legs, sew front and back of animal together. Stuff lightly. Insert arms as the side seams are sewn. Fold ears slightly at base and insert in head seam.

Gather neck slightly using yarn to match head color. Cut and sew felt features as in diagram, *right.* Embroider remaining facial details using six strands of embroidery floss. Stitch on black and white felt eyes with white embroidered highlights, a gold muzzle, and a black mouth and eyebrows.

For the rabbit

RABBIT FRONT: Follow bear directions through Row 22 using sea oats.

Row 23: With granite, k.

Rows 24-26: Work ribbing k1, p1.

Row 27: K 3, (p 1, k 2) 5 times; p 1, k 3.

Rows 28 and 30: P 3, (k 1, p 2) 5 times; k 1, p 3.

Row 29: K 3, (p 1, place next st on cable needle and hold in back, k next st, k st from cable needle, p 1, k 2) 3 times; k 1.

Rep Rows 27-30 four times more.

Rows 47-49: Work ribbing k1, p1. *Row 50:* Attach cranberry, p across.

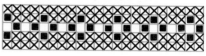

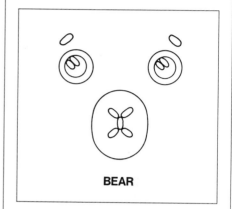

1 Square = 1 Stitch

⊠ **Dartmouth Green**
■ **Cranberry**
☐ **Sea Oats Heather**

BEAR

RABBIT

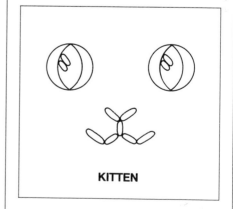

KITTEN

continued

Complete remaining front same as for bear front changing to sea oats for paws.

RABBIT BACK: Follow bear directions through Row 52.

RABBIT TAIL, *Row 1:* Sl 7 sts to holder; with sea oats, k next 8 sts; sl rem 7 sts to holder.
Rows 2-3: Work even.
Note: Work all rows not indicated in st st with no increases or decreases.
Rows 4 and 8: P, dec 1 st each side.
Rows 11 and 15: K, inc 1 st each side.
Work even through Row 18. Return all stitches to needle.
Row 53 of Back: With cranberry, k across all 22 sts.
Follow directions for bear back to complete back.

ARMS (make 2): With granite, cast on 22 sts. Work even in st st for 18 rows.
Rows 19-21: Work ribbing k1, p1.
Row 22: With sea oats, p across.
Rows 23-25: Work even.
Row 26: P 11 sts, sl rem st to stitch holder.
Rows 27 and 29: Working on 11 sts, k *and at same time,* dec 1 st each side.
Work through Row 30. Bind off 7 sts.
Work the opposite side of paw to correspond.

EARS (make 2): With mauve, cast on 10 sts. Work even for 7 rows.
Rows 8, 16, and 20: P, dec 1 st each side.
Row 23: Change to sea oats, k across.
Rows 25, 29, and 37: K, inc 1 st each side.
Work even through Row 44. Bind off 10 sts.

FINISHING: Attach body pieces as directed for bear. Add facial features following the pattern, page 45. Stitch on pink and red eyes with white embroidered highlights, and a gray mouth and eyebrows.

For the kitten
KITTEN FRONT: With granite, follow bear front directions through Row 22.
Row 23: With yellow, k across.
Row 24-26: Work ribbing k1, p 1. Work even through Row 42.
Rows 43-45: Work ribbing k1, p 1. *Row 46:* With white, p across.
Rows 47-56: Work even.
Row 57: K 11, sl rem 11 sts to stitch holder.
Row 59: With granite, k across.
Rows 60-71: Work even.
Row 72: With white, p across.
Rows 73-76: Work ribbing k 1, p 1. *Rows 77-78:* Work even.
Row 79: With black, k across.
Rows 80 and 82: Work even.
Rows 81 and 83: K, dec 1 st each side.
Row 84: P across. Bind off 7 sts. Work other leg to correspond.

KITTEN BACK: Work as for front through Row 52.

KITTEN TAIL, *Row 1:* Slip next 8 sts to stitch holder, with granite, k center 6 sts; sl rem 8 sts to holder.
Rows 2-26: Work even.
Row 27 and 29: K, dec 1 st each side.
Row 30 and 32: Work even.
Row 31 and 33: K, inc 1 st each side.
Work even for 26 more rows. Return all stitches to needle.
Row 53 of back: With white, k across 22 sts.
Complete back as for kitten front.

ARMS (make 2): With yellow, cast on 22 sts. Work even for 7 rows.
Rows 8-10: Work ribbing k 1, p 1.
Row 11: Change to granite, k across.
Work even through Row 25.
Row 26: P 11, sl rem 11 sts to holder.
Rows 27 and 29: Working on 11 sts, k, dec 1 st each side.
Rows 28 and 30: Work even. Bind off 7 sts.
Work other paw to correspond.

EARS (make 2): With mauve, cast on 12 sts.
Rows 1 and 2: Work even.
Note: All even rows, p; do not increase or decrease.
Rows 3, 5, 7, and 9: K, dec 1 st each side.
Row 11: Change to gray, k.
Rows 13, 15, 17, and 19: K, inc 1 st each side.
Work even through Row 21. Bind off 12 sts.

SKIRT FRONT: With cambridge, cast on 30 sts.
Rows 1-3: Work ribbing k 1, p 1.
Rows 4 and 6: P with yellow for stripes.
Row 5: With cambridge, k.
Rows 7, 9, 11, and 13: With cambridge, k, dec 1 st each side.
Rows 8, 10, 12, and 14: P with cambridge, do not inc or dec.
Row 15: Knit. Sl sts to holder.

SKIRT BACK: Work same as for skirt front. Sew side seams of skirt tog.
Finish body pieces same as for bear. Graft or sew the held stitches of skirt to bottom of kitten's sweater. Sew eyebrows using black carpet thread.
Add facial features following the pattern, page 45. Stitch on gold and black felt eyes with white embroidered highlights; embroider a pink nose and black mouth.

Changing Toys from Existing Patterns

While these animal toys will bring lots of joy to a very small child, you need not limit them to the colors we provide. For a more precious toy for an infant, work the bodies with white yarns and dress them in pastel clothing. Or, for a larger toy, knit them in worsted-weight yarns with size 7 or 8 needles, or in rug yarns with size 10 or 10½ needles. Dress them in colors to match a child's favorite outfit.

Heart and Alphabet Afghan

Shown on page 37.

Finished size is approximately 43x43 inches.

MATERIALS
Pingouin Pingofrance (50-gram balls): 8 balls ecru, 4 balls blue, 1 ball light rose
Size I afghan hook
Size G aluminum crochet hook

Abbreviations: See page 47.
Gauge: In afghan stitch, 20 sts = 5½ inches; 10 rows = 3 inches.

INSTRUCTIONS
BLOCKS (make 25): With ecru and afghan hook, ch 27.

Row 1 (first half): Insert hook in second ch from hook, yo, pull up lp and leave on hook, * insert hook in next ch, yo, pull up lp and leave on hook. Rep from * across—27 lps on hook.

Row 1 (second half): Yo, draw through 1 lp on hook, * yo, draw through 2 lps on hook. Rep from * across until 1 lp rem on hook.

Row 2 (first half): Sk first vertical bar of row below, * insert hook behind next vertical bar, yo, draw up lp and leave on hook. Rep from * across—27 lps on hook.

Row 2 (second half): Rep as for First Row, Second Half.

Rep Row 2 nineteen times more.

Bind-off row: Sk first vertical bar of row below, * insert hook behind next vertical bar, yo, draw lp through vertical bar and lp on hook—1 lp rem on hook. Rep from * across—21 rows. Do not fasten off.

Transfer lp to Size G hook and beg edging as follows: *Rnd 1:* Turn square to work along side of block, * sc in end of each of next 5 rows, 2 sc in end of next row. Rep from * 2 times more, 1 sc in end of each of last 3 rows; turn square to work along bottom edge; 3 sc in first st for corner, sc in next and each st to last st; 3 sc in last st for corner; turn square to work along next side of block, * sc in end of

each of next 5 rows, 2 sc in end of next row. Rep from * 2 times more; sc in end of each of last 3 rows; turn square to work along top edge of square; 3 sc in first st for corner, sc in next st and each st to last st, 3 sc in last st for corner; join with sl st to first sc. Fasten off ecru.

Rnd 2: Join blue with sc in second sc of any corner 3-sc-group, 2 sc in same sc; * work sc in each sc around, working 3 sc in center st of each 3-sc corner grp; join with sl st to beg sc.

Rnd 3: Ch 1, sc in same st as sl st, 3 sc in next sc; rep from * of Rnd 2. Fasten off. Block squares to equal size.

EMBROIDERY OF BLOCKS: Following graphs, *right,* work cross-stitches on blocks. Stitch 12 heart blocks. For the alphabet blocks, stitch pink-and-blue border (shown on chart) on rem 13 blocks. To complete the remaining letters of the alphabet, draw 24 5x5-square grids on graph paper and plot letters C through Z. Position two letters together as for the A-B square on the chart and work the embroidery.

ASSEMBLY: Lay out blocks in alphabetical order. Beg with the A-B block, make 5 strips of 5 blocks, alternating an alphabet block with a heart block. Sew squares into strips with a whipstitch in the *back* loops and whipstitch the strips tog.

BORDER, *Rnd 1:* Join blue with a sl st in second sc of any corner 3 sc-group, ch 4, dc in same st as sl st, * ch 1, sk next sc, dc in next sc. Rep from * around entire afghan, and at same time, work (dc, ch 1, dc) in center sc of each corner 3 sc-group; ending with ch 1, sl st in third ch of beg ch-4.

Rnd 2: Ch 2, in first ch-1 sp work (dc, trc, dc, hdc); sc in next ch-1 lp, * in next ch-1 sp work (hdc, dc, trc, dc, hdc); sc in next ch-1 sp. Rep from * around afghan, ending with a sl st in top of ch-2 at beg of rnd. Fasten off. Weave in yarn ends.

Abbreviations

beg	begin(ning)
ch	chain
dc	double crochet
dec	decrease
dp	double pointed
dtr	double treble
hdc	half-double crochet
inc	increase
k	knit
lp(s)	loop(s)
MC	main color
p	purl
pat	pattern
psso	pass slip st over
rem	remaining
rep	repeat
rnd	round
sc	single crochet
sk	skip
sl st	slip stitch
sp	space
st(s)	stitch(es)
st st	stockinette stitch
tog	together
yo	yarn over
*	repeat from * as indicated

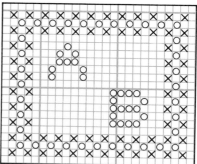

COLOR KEY
⊠ **Light Rose**
▢ **Blue**

COVERLETS

FOR CARRIAGE AND CRADLE

In this special coverlet chapter, you'll find a variety of stitchery techniques, including pieced and appliquéd quilts and embroidered and machine-stitched designs. Instructions for all the coverlets begin on page 54.

Besides being a welcome and warm accessory for babies, a coverlet is a great way to learn the art of patchwork and quilting. Because the size is smaller than a conventional quilt, obtaining good results is quicker. And because crib coverlets are made in a more manageable size, all the quilting can be worked on the machine, replacing tedious hand-quilting.

An embroidered panel forms the center of the Victorian-style coverlet, *left.* The panel features a wicker pram, nursery toys, and a pair of lovebirds. Outlined hearts, stitched in pretty pastels, form the border.

The panel is set into a light print background and edged with a darker print ruffle and gathered eyelet. More eyelet and a piped edge form the outer ruffle. The coverlet is tuft-quilted on the fabric background, and outline-quilted around the embroidered toys.

Fancy machine embroidery stitches are the key to the super-simple quilt, *opposite.*

Begin this stitchery project with a long strip of plain fabric. Then work closely spaced rows of stitches in different designs and colors and cut the strip into squares.

Assemble the quilt with four lettered squares, a ruffly edging, and extra-loft batting for added puffiness.

The menagerie of embroidered animals used for the patchwork coverlet, *right,* was inspired by an antique tablecloth designed for a child.

The center panel is made of embroidered squares, each with a different animal, and blocks pieced with four calico triangles. Border strips complete the top.

Any of the coverlets featured in this chapter can be made with alternate motifs or patterns, enabling you to put your own stamp of individuality on your creation.

Sources of good designs for quilts and coverlets are all around you, so don't hesitate to be a creative stitcher.

Look through children's books or magazines with juvenile illustrations for inspiration for motifs. Or let the baby's older brother or sister create an original piece of artwork and interpret it in embroidery or appliqué for a one-of-a-kind quilt.

You can often find inexpensive old needlework pattern books at flea markets or in antique shops. These usually feature sweet designs for embroidery and other needlework designs that are ideal for infant accessories.

Substitute a favorite quilt pattern for the Dresden Plate coverlet shown on page 52. Or, in the album quilt tradition, provide friends and family with fabric and dimensions and have them each contribute a block.

Dresden Plate is the name of the familiar patchwork pattern used for the pastel coverlet, *above.* Sixteen blue and pink wedges are stitched together for each motif, and the assembly is appliquéd to a white block.

The unusual border is stitched from white triangles and rounded print wedges. Three adjacent wedges makes the neat corners.

Because a lot of background is available, quilting possibilities are varied, from simple lines as shown to more intricate patterns.

Garlands of simple lotus blossoms and leaves are used for the unusual coverlet, *opposite.* The technique used is candlewicking, and it couldn't be easier to do. Just sketch the design onto the fabric, and stitch rows of evenly spaced French knots along the lines.

A crib pillow shares the same motif.

To adapt this design for a larger coverlet, simply repeat more borders until the coverlet is the desired size, or set a panel into the center of other fabric.

Embroidered and Tied Coverlet

Shown on pages 48–49.

The finished coverlet measures 29x33 inches, excluding ruffle.

MATERIALS
⅔ yard of 44-inch-wide medium-weight white fabric
1 yard print fabric for top
1½ yards print fabric for backing, cording, and ruffle
One skein *each* of embroidery floss in the following colors: peach, yellow, lavender, light blue, pink, gray, brown, and gold metallic; two skeins light green
2 yards of 2-inch-wide gathered white eyelet
4 yards of 3-inch-wide gathered white eyelet
4 yards of narrow cotton cording
Pearl cotton or crochet thread for tying the coverlet
Quilt batting
16x18-inch piece of polyester fleece
Water-erasable pen

INSTRUCTIONS
Note: Instructions allow for a ½-inch seam allowance.
Preshrink all of the fabrics and cording. From the white fabric, cut a piece for the lining measuring 16x18 inches; set aside.

EMBROIDERED BLOCK: Enlarge the pattern, *opposite,* onto graph paper. Use water-erasable pen to transfer the design onto the remaining piece of white fabric. Center the design on the fabric to allow 2 inches beyond the pattern on all sides.
Using three strands of embroidery floss and referring to the color key, *opposite,* work satin stitches in the following areas: the ribbon; breasts, wings, and tails of birds; arms, ears, and bow of the bear; the horse rocker, saddle, and heart; two sides of each block; the curved framework of carriage; small circles on carriage wheels; and leaves between the hearts on the border.

Work French knots on small circles between the long stitches on the carriage body and umbrella covering. Work the remaining areas in outline stitches. (Work outline stitches around the areas filled with satin stitches.)
When the embroidery is completed, trim the fabric to 16x18 inches. Lightly press on wrong side, using a press cloth.
Place the polyester fleece between the wrong sides of the embroidered piece and the piece of white lining fabric; baste the layers together. Quilt around the birds, bow, carriage, and horse with white quilting thread. Quilt heart shapes with pastel shades of floss. Remove the basting stitches.
With right sides together, baste the 2-inch-wide eyelet around the embroidered piece.
From the backing fabric, cut four strips, each 5x44 inches. Sew strips together end to end, to make a large circle. With wrong sides together, fold circle in half lengthwise. Gather raw edges to fit around the embroidered piece. With right sides facing, sew ruffle atop the eyelet trim. Set this piece aside.

CORDING: Cut four strips, each ¾x44 inches, from the backing fabric. Join into one long strip; cover the cotton cording.

COVERLET TOP AND BACKING: Cut top piece to measure 30x34 inches. With right sides together, sew the piping then the gathered 3-inch eyelet to the outside edges.
Cut quilt batting slightly larger than top and baste to wrong side of top.
Cut the backing slightly larger than the quilt top. With right sides together, sew the top and back of coverlet together, leaving an opening for turning; trim, clip corners, turn.

FINISHING: Using two strands of crochet thread or pearl cotton, tie the quilt in rows 2 inches apart and at 2-inch intervals. Center the embroidered piece atop the tied coverlet and hand-sew in place, leaving the ruffled edges free.

Embroidered Animal Quilt

Shown on page 51.

The finished size is 34x29 inches, excluding the ruffle.

MATERIALS
1⅛ yards of 44-inch-wide red print fabric for backing and outside sashing strips
½ yard of 44-inch-wide blue print fabric for sashing strips
½ yard of 44-inch-wide white cotton fabric
¼ yard *each* of two 44-inch-wide red and white print fabrics—one predominantly red, the other predominantly white
Quilt batting
3⅔ yards of gathered 3½-inch-wide eyelet
2½ yards of ⅜-inch-wide gros-grain ribbon
Red embroidery floss
Quilting thread
Water-erasable pen

INSTRUCTIONS
Note: Instructions allow for a ¼-inch seam allowance. The finished blocks measure 5¼ inches square.

ANIMAL BLOCKS: On the white fabric, draw ten 5¾-inch squares. Do not cut out until all embroidery is completed. Enlarge the animal patterns, page 56, onto the graph paper. With the water-erasable pen, trace the patterns onto the blocks. Using outline stitches, work the outlines of the animals with three strands of floss. Use French knots and satin stitches as desired for other embroidery embellishments. Cut the blocks from the fabric.

continued

1 Square = 1 Inch

COLOR KEY:

1 Light Green	4 Lavender	7 Gray
2 Peach	5 Light Blue	8 Gold Metallic
3 Yellow	6 Pink	9 Brown

COVERLETS

1 Square = 1 Inch

TRIANGLE BLOCK: Make a triangular template by drawing a 5¼-inch square onto cardboard. Draw an X through the center of the square; cut square apart into 4 equal triangles. Add ¼ inch around all sides of one of the triangular sections and use this section as pattern template. Cut 20 triangles from *each* of the red and white print fabrics (40 total). Make 10 squares from the triangles alternating the red and white prints as you piece them together.

ASSEMBLY OF BLOCKS: Baste and sew the 20 blocks together, alternating the embroidered and pieced squares. Make five strips, *each* containing four blocks; sew strips together.

SASHING STRIPS: From the blue fabric, cut four sashing strips as follows: two measuring 3x32¼ inches and two measuring 3x27 inches. Sew these strips to the quilt top, leaving 3-inch extensions on each end; miter the corners.

Cut four red sashing strips as follows: two measuring 2x36¼ inches and two measuring 2x31 inches. Piece these strips to the blue borders on the quilt top, allowing 2-inch extensions on each end; miter the corners.

FINISHING: Cut quilt backing (from red fabric) and batting to measure 33x38 inches. On a flat surface, layer the quilt pieces as follows: the backing (wrong side up), the batting, and the quilt top (right side up). Make sure the backing and the batting extend 2 inches around on all sides. Baste all layers together.

Beginning at the center, quilt around the inside edges of the animal squares, and quilt an X design in the triangle squares. Quilt along the inside edges of the blue sashing strip.

Baste and sew eyelet ruffle to the quilt top *only*. Trim excess batting and backing to allow a ½-inch seam allowance. Turn under seam allowance and whipstitch to quilt top to finish.

Decorative Machine-Stitched Coverlet

Shown on page 50.

The finished size is approximately 30x24 inches, excluding the ruffle.

MATERIALS
¾ yard of 45-inch-wide neutral fabric for quilt top
¾ yard printed fabric for backing
4 yards of 1½ inch-wide gathered cotton lace
¾ yard 44-inch-wide pink fabric
½ yard 44-inch-wide blue fabric
Pastel machine embroidery thread
Quilt batting; water-erasable pen

INSTRUCTIONS
Note: Instructions allow for a ½-inch seam allowance.

QUILT TOP: From the neutral fabric, cut a strip of fabric 45x11 inches. Starting 1 inch from the raw edge, with the water-erasble pen, draw 10 parallel lines 1 inch apart across the 45-inch width. Select decorative stitches on your sewing machine and stitch on the marked lines, changing thread colors on each line. Cut five blocks from this strip, each measuring 9x11 inches.

Cut four additional blocks, each measuring 9x11 inches, from the remaining neutral piece of fabric. Using the photograph as a guide, draw letters (A, B, C, D) on each of these four blocks with the water-erasable pen. Machine-stitch over these letters using decorative stitches.

Alternating the decorative and the alphabet blocks, piece three blocks together to make one strip; make two more strips. Piece the strips together; press seams to one side.

With right sides together, baste the cotton lace around the edges of the quilt top.

RUFFLE: From pink fabric, cut five strips, each measuring 5x44 inches; sew the strips together to make one piece. From the blue fabric, cut five strips each measuring 2½x44 inches; sew strips together to make one piece.

With the right sides together, join blue and pink strips along one long edge. Sew the short ends together to make a circle. With wrong sides together, fold strip in half, raw edges even; press.

With yellow thread, sew a decorative stitch on the pink edge on right side (pink and blue) of the ruffle. Gather to fit the quilt top. With the right sides of ruffle and quilt top facing, baste ruffle in place atop the lace edging.

QUILT BACKING: Cut the quilt backing and the batting slightly larger than the quilt top. Baste the batting to the wrong side of the backing.

ASSEMBLY: With right sides of the top and back facing, machine-stitch around the sides of the quilt, leaving a 12-inch opening to turn. (Pin the ruffle back on the quilt top so it does not catch in the seam.) Clip the edges and turn. Hand-sew the opening to close.

To complete, machine-stitch in the seams around the blocks.

Decorative Machine-Stitching Tips

For the finest looking finish on projects embellished with decorative machine stitching, pad the fabric before you begin. Cut polyester fleece to equal the finished size of the piece you are working on, and baste it to the wrong side.

If the fleece slides on the feed dogs on the machine, place notebook paper underneath it. Tear away the paper when you complete the machine embroidery.

Also, practice stitching on a fabric scrap backed with fleece to check the thread tension. When the tension is correct, the stitches will lie flat and smooth on both sides of the fabric.

COVERLETS

Dresden Plate Baby Quilt

Shown on page 52.

Finished size is 43x59½ inches.

MATERIALS
Assorted blue and pink fabric
  scraps
2 yards of 45-inch-wide white
  cotton fabric
1¾ yards of 45-inch-wide
  backing fabric
Quilt batting
Quilting thread
Plastic or cardboard material for
  template.

INSTRUCTIONS
Note: Instructions allow for a
¼-inch seam allowance unless
otherwise specified.
  Trace patterns, *below,* for the
Dresden Plate wedge and the inner and outer border triangles.

Add ¼-inch seam allowances to
all the edges; cut shapes from
plastic or cardboard to make templates. Cut a 5-inch-diameter
circle from cardboard for center of
motifs. (This measurement includes a ⅛-inch seam allowance.)

  DRESDEN PLATE BLOCKS:
Preshrink all fabrics. On wrong
side of fabrics, trace around templates with a soft-lead pencil,
matching arrows on pattern
pieces to straight grain of fabric.
  Trace and cut out a total of 48
pink wedges and 48 blue wedges.
For border, trace and cut 34 pink
outer border wedges and 34 blue
outer border wedges.
  From the white fabric, cut out
six 16½-inch white squares, and
60 white inner border triangles;
trace and cut 6 circles.
  For each quilt block, arrange
16 Dresden Plate wedges, alternating blue and pink wedges. Beginning at the narrow end of each

wedge, piece them together along
seam line. Do not stitch into the
seam allowance at the outside
edge (this step will ease the finishing of the outside edge). Press
seams to one side.
  Fold under the outside curved
edges of the plate. Center, baste,
and hand-appliqué the plate to
the background square.
  On circles, turn under ⅛ inch;
press and appliqué to the center
of the plate motif.
  Piece quilt blocks together making two 2 strips, each with three
blocks. Piece strips together.

  BORDER: Alternating blue and
pink outer wedges between white
inner triangles, piece sufficient
border wedges to extend along
each side of the quilt top. Do not
stitch into the seam allowance at
the outside edge. At corners, eliminate white triangles. Piece 3 outer border pieces together to turn
corner. Sew border to quilt's top.

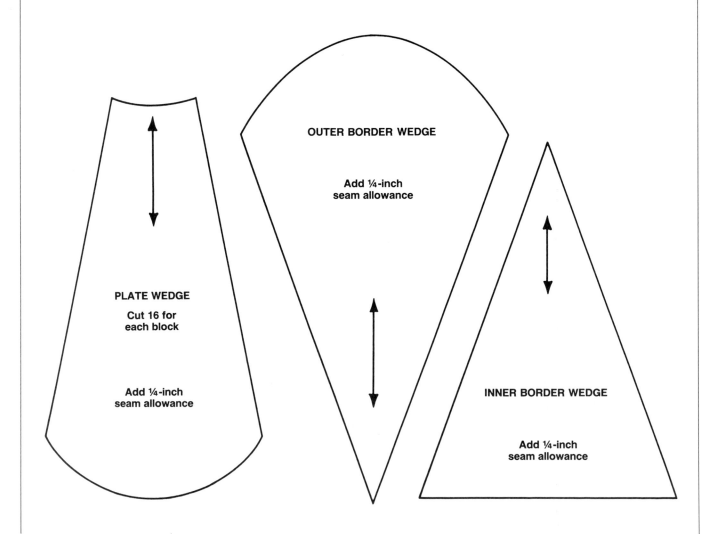

PLATE WEDGE

Cut 16 for
each block

Add ¼-inch
seam allowance

OUTER BORDER WEDGE

Add ¼-inch
seam allowance

INNER BORDER WEDGE

Add ¼-inch
seam allowance

ASSEMBLY: Baste three layers together as follows: the backing, wrong side up; the batting; the pieced top, right side up. Hand-quilt as desired.

Trim batting to ¼ inch smaller than quilt top. Press under raw edges ¼ inch on top. Trim backing to fit top, turn under raw edges and slip-stitch closed. Edges may also be finished with bias-cut strips.

French Knot Baby Coverlet

Shown on page 53.

The finished size is approximately 36x44 inches.

MATERIALS
2¾ yards of 44-inch-wide white cotton for top and backing
1⅓ yards of 44-inch white cotton flannel
3 skeins cotton knit and crochet thread
4¾ yards of 2-inch-wide gathered cotton lace
Water-erasable pen
Embroidery or quilting hoop

INSTRUCTIONS
Preshrink all fabrics. Enlarge design onto graph paper. Cut fabric into two pieces, each measuring 40x48 inches for the quilt top and lining back.

COVERLET TOP: Tape or pin top piece atop the enlarged pattern and trace the design using the water-erasable pen. Flop the pattern to make mirror images in all quadrants.

Cut and baste the flannel to the wrong side of the top piece. Place fabric in hoop and work the entire design using French knot stitches. Work the outline of the border first; then work stems, leaves, and berries of border. In the center of the design, work the outline of the circle, then proceed to the stems of the flowers. Complete embroidery by working the leaves and flowers.

Rinse coverlet in cool water and allow to dry. Trim coverlet edge to

1 Square = 1 Inch

½ inch from the outside border.

With the right sides together, baste the cotton lace to the outside edges using a ¼-inch seam allowance.

LINING AND ASSEMBLY: Cut the backing piece to fit the quilt top. With right sides together, pin the backing to the quilt top. Sew around the coverlet using basting threads as a guide; leave a 10-inch opening for turning. Clip and trim corners; turn and press. Slip-stitch opening closed.

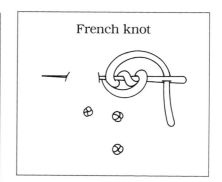

French knot

TEDDY BEAR CHRISTMAS

TRIMS AND TOYS

Children, teddy bears, and Christmas are a combination that just can't miss. To prove the point, here (and on the next two pages) are delightful teddy bear projects to make for baby and your holiday home. Work the designs in a variety of craft techniques, from woodworking to appliqué to cross-stitching. Instructions begin on page 64.

Fill the adorable stocking, *above*, with all kinds of goodies for a memorable treat on baby's first Christmas morning.

The teddy bear and tree motifs are appliquéd to the stocking background and trimmed with bright metallic touches—tiny gold stitches on the bear and garlands of beads on the tree.

Dressed for a romp in the snow, the cuddly teddy toy, *left*, is sure to become a lifelong friend.

The bear is stitched from tan woolen fabric, with brown corduroy on the paws and feet. Purchased glass eyes, a stitched-on vinyl nose, and an embroidered mouth complete his winsome expression. Because the bear's arms and legs are securely jointed, they can move freely.

The quick-to-knit sweater, cap, and muffler dress up this bear in wintry style. The sweater is designed to fit the bear's contours and is made with raglan sleeves and a turtleneck. Use bits of leftover yarn for the ribbed muffler and matching stocking hat.

Few dough creations have the spirited personality of the dough bear Christmas ornaments shown here and on the two previous pages.

These charming characters are created from clay that's a simple concoction of flour, salt, and water. The addition of instant tea granules tints the dough to just the right color for bears. Other colored portions are painted with acrylics.

To make the bears permanent, they're slow-baked in an oven.

Pindot fabric is the perfect choice for the bears *at right*.

To make these ornaments, cut the bear shape from both fabric and fusible webbing. Fuse the fabric to a piece of felt backing and then outline with machine-satin stitches. Add hand-embroidered features and trim away the backing.

Designed especially for tiny hands to manipulate, the tree and teddy puzzle, *right*, is an ideal stocking stuffer for little ones.

The shape is drawn onto pine scraps and cut out with a jigsaw. Diluted acrylic paints add the color. To make the puzzle more challenging for older kids, cut it into additional pieces.

For more Christmas puzzle ideas for children, consider greeting cards, wrapping papers, calendars, and other illustrated materials for design ideas.

Tiny stitcheries such as the cross-stitch teddy ornaments, *opposite*, deserve prominent display on the tree. This ornament is decorated with motifs adapted from traditional cross-stitched samplers.

Because the bears are stitched over only one thread of hardanger fabric, detailed motifs can be worked into the design. To make this ornament into a small toy, stitch on fabrics with a smaller thread count or stitch over two or three threads of hardanger fabric.

1 Square = 1 Inch

Appliquéd Stocking

Shown on page 60.

Finished size is 8¼ inches long.

MATERIALS
⅓ yard fabric for stocking
¼ yard contrasting fabric for cuff, piping, and drum appliqué
¼ yard lining fabric
12x10-inch piece of batting
Scrap of green fabric for tree
Scrap of brown fabric for bear and tree trunk; scrap of ecru fabric for drum top
Light yellow, pink, cream, and metallic embroidery floss
Small beads for eye and nose
1-inch star appliqué for treetop
½ yard narrow lace trim
Graph paper; water-erasable pen
Narrow cotton cording

INSTRUCTIONS
Enlarge pattern, *above*. With water-erasable pen, trace stocking shape and placement of appliqués on the stocking fabric. Do not cut out stocking until appliqué and embroidery are complete.

Trace and cut out the appliqué pieces from fabrics; allow ¼-inch seam allowance. Hand-appliqué to stocking.

Satin-stitch the bear's nose with cream floss and inner ear with pink. With yellow, outline-stitch bear's body parts. Add beads for eye and nose. Accent tree with gold metallic French knots. Using outline and back stitches, define drum with metallic floss. Sew star to treetop.

Machine-sew batting to wrong side of stocking on seam line; cut out, leaving ½-inch seam margin. Cut stocking back to match front.

Cover cording using contrasting fabric. Sew cording to stocking front; clip curves. With right sides facing, sew back to front, leaving top open. Trim seam, clip curves, turn, and press.

Cut two stocking pieces from lining fabric, adding ¼-inch seam allowance. Sew pieces together, right sides facing. Slip lining into stocking, baste along top edge.

Cut cuff and cuff lining from contrasting fabric, adding ¼-inch seam margin. (Cuff is one continuous piece with one seam at side.) On right side of cuff, sew lace to scallops; clip curves.

With right sides facing, sew scalloped edge of cuff and lining. Clip curves. Open lining; sew side seams, right sides facing.

Keeping cuff lining free, place cuff inside stocking; sew straight edge of cuff to stocking. Pull cuff out of stocking. Turn under seam margin of lining; hand-sew atop seam allowance. Turn cuff over.

Teddy Bear

Shown on page 61.

MATERIALS
½ yard camel-colored wool flannel; 8x10-inch scrap of brown corduroy for paws and soles; small piece of dark brown vinyl for nose
Black embroidery floss
Glass eyes
Fiberfill; dressmaker's carbon
4-inch length of 1-inch-diameter wood dowel
Four 2-inch-long cotter pins
Brunswick Pomfret 50-gram balls: 2 balls No. 512 royal blue (MC), 1 ball No. 500 white
Size 5 knitting needles
Four stitch markers

Abbreviations: See page 47.
Gauge: 6 sts = 1 inch; 8 rows = 1 inch

INSTRUCTIONS
Note: Pattern includes ¼-inch seam allowances.

Enlarge pattern, *opposite*. Fold fabric in half and cut pattern pieces. Mark eye and ear placements, and points of attachments for arms and legs. Cut soles and paws (lower portion of arm pattern) from brown corduroy.

With right sides facing, pin body front and back pieces together. Sew along center front and back seams; sew side seams.

With right sides facing, pin and stitch leg pieces, leaving openings at top and bottom. Pin and stitch soles to bottoms of legs; turn.

Turn under straight edge of paw and stitch to two arm pieces (for inner arms). Pin and stitch inner arms to outer arm pieces, leaving openings at top. Trim seams and turn.

Make eight wooden washers by slicing the wooden dowel into ¼-inch-thick discs; sand. Drill a ⅛-inch-diameter hole in center of each disc.

Attach arms and legs as follows: Place one wooden disc on inside of body. Insert one cotter pin through hole in disc, through fabric of body where marked, through fabric of arm or leg as marked. Slide a second wooden disc onto cotter pin and bend prongs apart to secure limb.

Stuff trunk, arms, and legs. Hand-sew openings, except neck edge, closed.

Stitch darts on side head pieces. With right sides facing, stitch head center to head sides from back neck edge to nose. Stitch head side pieces from center front neck to nose; turn.

Attach eyes by pushing the eye shank through fabric and secure with fasteners. Stuff head firmly.

Cut an equilateral triangle (1⅛-inch sides) from vinyl for nose and round off corners. Place stuffing under nose and hand-sew over point where seams meet. Refer to photograph, page 61, and embroider mouth with six strands of embroidery floss.

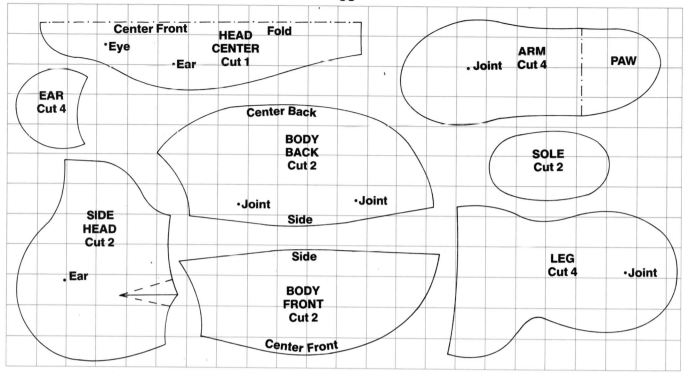

1 Square = 1 Inch

With right sides facing, sew ears; leave bottom open. Turn; stuff. Turn under raw edges; slip-stitch closed. Attach to head as marked. Turn under raw edges of neck edge; pin head to body at center front and back, matching shoulder seams with head darts; slip-stitch in place.

For the sweater

BACK: With MC cast on 36 sts. Work in k 1, p 1 rib for 5 rows. Change to st st, inc 14 sts on first row—50 sts. Work even until total length measures 1¾ inches ending with a wrong-side row.

ARMHOLE SHAPING: Bind off 9 sts at beg of next 2 rows. Work even on rem 32 sts until length from beg of armhole shaping measures ¾ inch, ending with a wrong-side row.

STRIPE PATTERN: Work next 2 rows in white. *Next row:* * K 2 with white, k 1 MC. Rep from * ending k 2 with white. Work 2 more rows with white. Change to MC and work even until the length from beg of armhole shaping is 2½ inches, end with a wrong-side row.

NECK SHAPING: K 7 for left shoulder, sl rem 25 sts to holder.

Dec 1 st at neck edge every other row twice. Work even on rem 5 sts until length from beg of armhole shaping measures 3¾ inches. Bind off. Keeping center 18 sts on holder for Back neck, shape rem 7 sts of right shoulder as for left shoulder.

FRONT: Work as for Back until length from beg of armhole shaping measures 2 inches, ending with a wrong-side row. K 10 for left shoulder; sl rem 22 sts to holder. Dec 1 st at neck edge every other row 5 times. Work even on rem 5 sts until length from beg of armhole shaping measures 3¾ inches. Bind off. Keeping center 12 sts on holder for Front neck, shape rem 10 sts for right shoulder as for left shoulder. Bind off.

SLEEVES (make 2): Cast on 24 sts. Work in k 1, p 1 rib for 5 rows. Change to st st, inc 16 sts on first row. Work even until total length is 2¼ inches, end on wrong side. Work 5 rows stripe pat. When total length is 3¾ inches, mark beg and end of row for armholes. Work even in MC until total length is 5¼ inches, ending with a wrong-side row. Bind off.

FINISHING: Sew right shoulder. Beg at left shoulder, with MC and right side facing, pick up 11

sts along Front neck edge, work 12 sts from Front holder, pick up 11 sts along other Front edge, pick up 6 sts along Back neck edge, work 18 sts from Back neck holder, pick up 6 sts along rem Back neck edge—64 sts. Work in k 1, p 1 rib for 16 rows. Bind off.

Sew shoulder and neck seam. Sew bound-off edge of sleeve to Front and Back armhole. Sew edges of sleeves from markers to Front and Back armhole bound off edges. Sew rem seams.

For the ski cap

With MC, cast on 60 sts. Work in k 1, p 1 rib for 8 rows. Change to st st, work 6 rows, inc 15 sts on first row—75 sts. Cont in st st, work 5 rows of stripe pattern; Work 7 rows even in MC.

Next row (right side): K 2 tog across row, end k 1—38 sts rem. P 2 tog across—19 sts. K 2 tog across, end k 1—10 sts rem. Break off. Draw end through rem sts. Pull tightly and fasten; sew back seam. Make pom-pom with white yarn. Sew to cap.

For the scarf

With white, cast on 11 sts.
Work k 1, p 1 rib for 8 rows.
(* *Next row*: With blue, knit across. *Following row*: With blue, work in ribbing as established.

continued

Change to white and rep from * for next 2 rows. Change to blue and rep from * for next 2 rows. Change to white, k 1 row.) Continue in ribbing with white until total length measures 20 inches; end with wrong-side row. Rep bet ( )'s. Cont in rib for 7 rows more. Bind off.

Wooden Puzzle

Shown on page 62.

MATERIALS
Scraps of ¾-inch pine
Acrylic paints; clear varnish

INSTRUCTIONS
Enlarge the pattern, *below.* Transfer shapes to pine. Cut out pieces; sand. Paint designs onto wood. When dry, varnish to seal.

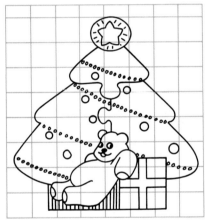

1 Square = 1 Inch

Appliquéd Bears

Shown on pages 62–63.

Ornaments are 5¼ inches tall.

MATERIALS
9x12-inch piece of green felt (to make four ornaments)
Scraps of brown or red pindot fabric and black floss
Thread to match the fabrics
Fusible webbing
Dressmaker's carbon paper

1 Square = 1 Inch

INSTRUCTIONS
Note: No seam allowances are necessary on this pattern.
Enlarge pattern, *above.* For each ornament, cut one bear from fabric and one from fusible webbing. Place bear right side up (webbing underneath), atop felt. Place a paper towel over the ornament and fuse fabrics together.
Machine-satin-stitch along the raw edges of the appliqué to secure the fabric to the felt.
Using dressmaker's carbon, transfer dotted lines from pattern to ornament; define lines with machine satin stitches. Work black French knots for eyes.
Cut bear from felt, leaving ⅛-inch-wide borders around. Tack a loop of embroidery floss to top of ornament for hanging.

Dough Bear Ornaments

Shown on pages 62-63.

MATERIALS
1 cup flour; ¼ cup salt
Instant tea; acrylic paints
Food coloring
India ink; fine-point pen
Watercolor paintbrush
Small safety pins; paper clips
Scraps of nylon net; pinecones
Macrame wood block; varnish

INSTRUCTIONS
Mix dry ingredients with 6 tablespoons of *hot water.* Dough should be soft, not sticky. Separate dough into balls to color. For bodies, add 2 tablespoons instant tea per cup of flour. Use food colors to make clothing and other colored trims. Knead until dough feels smooth.

For flat ornaments
Form body parts by rolling small amounts of dough in palms and shaping it. Moisten dough with water where pieces touch.
For hangers, clip U-shaped part of a paper clip; insert in ornament before baking. Bake at 275 degrees for 2½ hours. Ornaments are done when they are hard; cool. Draw faces with India ink and a fine point pen. For cheeks, use a wash of red paint. Varnish.

For three-dimensional ornaments
Form body; attach to pinecone or block. Bake 15 minutes at 275 degrees. Add head and legs. Bake 15 minutes; cool. Add arms, bake 15 minutes; cool. Add ears, bows, or other finishing details. Bake an hour or until done.

For bows
Shape and press a diamond; fold in half to make half of bow. Repeat for other side. Make another diamond; cut in half diagonally (ties). Add small ball of dough for knot.

For diaper
Add diaper shape before attaching legs. Add a triangle with safety pin slipped over it. Add legs.

For skater
Use half of paper clip for blade.

For ballerinas
Cut a 1¼x14 inch strip of net. Sew running stitches down middle to gather and fit around body. Glue to bear when varnish is dry.

For wreath
Twist two 6-inch dough strips into a circle. Place on bear; position arms. Cover joint with bow.

For bear in stocking

Use whole cloves for eyes. Push dough through garlic press for fur trim.

Cross-stitched Bear Ornaments

Shown on pages 62-63.

Ornament is 5½ inches tall.

MATERIALS

6x8-inch piece of hardanger to make one ornament
Embroidery floss in desired colors (see Color Key, *below, right*)
6x44-inches of calico fabric for backing and piping
Water-erasable pen
Cotton cording; graph paper

INSTRUCTIONS

Transfer chart, *right*, to graph paper. Make a mirror image of the bear to the right of the center line. The lettering and placement of "Teddy" is indicated on the chart.

The ornaments shown on pages 62-63 are stitched with the six colors listed in the color key, but the placement of the colors varies for each bear.

When embroidery is complete, draw the bear outline to scale as shown, *right*, and make a tissue paper pattern. Center and transfer the tissue pattern to the cross-stitched bear with water-erasable pen. Baste along the traced line.

Cover cotton cording with the calico to make piping. Baste, then machine-stitch the piping to the bear front one thread outside the basting line. Clip the curves and finger-press the seam allowance to the back side.

Trace and cut the shape of the bear onto the calico fabric. Stay-stitch on the seam line around the outside edges. Clip curves and turn under raw edges; baste.

Slip-stitch the calico backing to the piping of the bear front, leaving an opening for stuffing.

Stuff bear; slip-stitch the opening closed. Tack a loop of embroidery floss to the top of ornament for hanging.

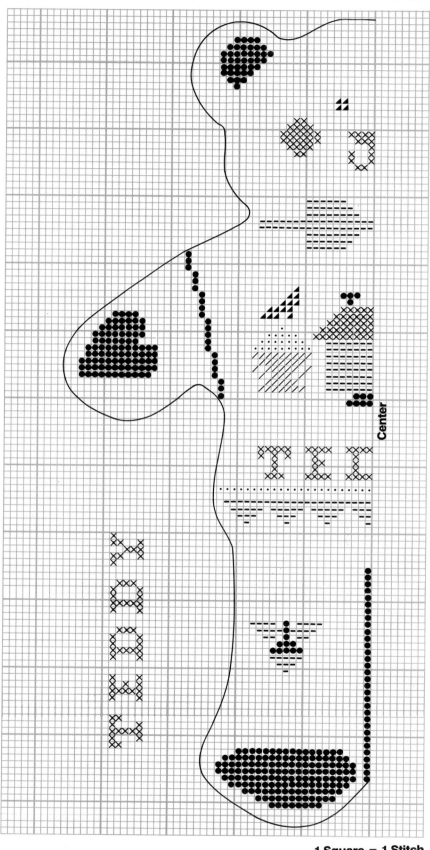

1 Square = 1 Stitch

COLOR KEY

⊡ Yellow	⊟ Green	⧄ Peach
◉ Brown	⊠ Red	⧄ Blue

MOTHER GOOSE DESIGNS

◆ ◆ ◆

Come join Mother Goose and her cast of characters in this chapter's selection of nursery accessories. You'll find your childhood favorites on quilts, toys, and clothing. Instructions for these projects begin on page 74.

Mother Goose and six of her friends form the inspiration for our nursery collection.

The patchwork crib quilt *at left* features several different types of patchwork and quilt-making techniques. The center panel portrays Mother Goose on one of her story-telling journeys. Smaller blocks portray Mary and her lamb, Little Bo-Peep, Wee Willie Winkie, the Ten-O'Clock Scholar, Polly with her kettle, and Tom, the Piper's Son.

The character blocks are cut from muslin, with the outlines drawn on using permanent markers. Delicate washes of acrylic paints and touches of embroidery add color.

The remaining quilt blocks are pieced in the nine-patch pattern or appliquéd with simple hearts. Fabric strips embroidered with a Mother Goose rhyme form the border.

Make a child's garment extra-special with easy painted-on designs such as the pinafore and romper, *opposite.*

The muslin pinafore was made from a commercial pattern and the nursery character was painted onto the fabric before assembly. The romper bib was similarly painted, and more durable fabric was used for the pant legs. Painting the design onto a purchased plain-colored dress, jumper, or pair of overalls would work equally well.

As with the quilt featured on pages 68–69 and other projects throughout this chapter, the painted figures are accented with simple embroidery stitches, and the pinafore features an embroidered verse.

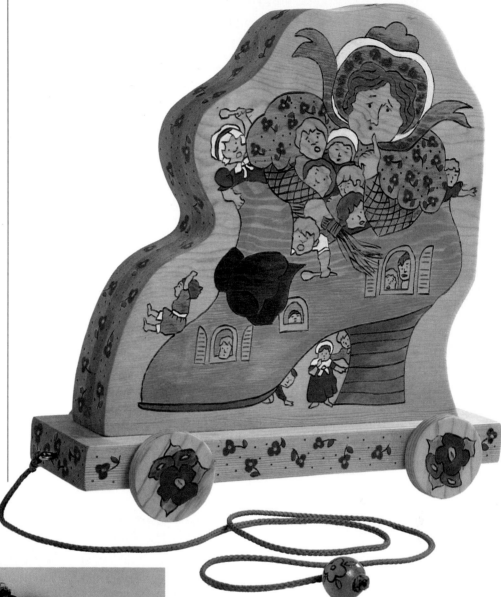

Just a single flower motif (from the nursery rhyme character motif borders) is used for the appliquéd tote bag, *left.* The generously sized tote is more than adequate for bottles, diapers, and toys.

Machine-appliqué is used for the flower motifs on the pocket, which is hand-quilted in a grid pattern. To simplify the job, substitute prequilted fabric for the pocket.

Few pull toys are as original and as fun as the Old Woman in a Shoe toy, *above.*

The pattern is first woodburned onto a scrap of pine and colored with acrylic paints. Then the design is cut out in a safely rounded shape and mounted onto a wooden base. Wheels are cut from pine scraps. As with all of the projects in this chapter, any of the larger motifs can be used for this toy design.

A special clay recipe used for the Wee Willie Winkie wall plaque, *left*, is easy to sculpt and extra-durable. The clay is equal parts of flour and salt, with enough water added to hold the mixture together.

Begin the plaque with a large outline of any of the Mother Goose characters, and shape each portion using the outline as a guide. When the plaque is completed, dry it for a few hours in a warm oven. Decorate the figure with bright acrylic paints, and protect it with several coats of clear finish.

The simple shaped pillows, *opposite*, are painted on muslin and decorated with embroidery, trims, and other small notions.

Transfer the outlines onto muslin with a dark brown permanent marker. Fill in the areas with diluted acrylic paints. Then add embroidery and other accents. Wee Willie Winkie, for example, is embellished with rickrack trim on his nightshirt and a couched-down drawstring. Mary's lamb is textured with French knots, and her dress features flower appliqués and ribbons.

Familiar nursery stories are woodburned into the sides of the toy box, *right*. The shenanigans of the Three Men in a Tub, Peter Pumpkin-Eater, and the Old Woman in a Shoe are shown here, with the Mother Goose motif from the quilt on pages 68–69 on the fourth side.

The sides of the box are cut from pine and decorated before the box is assembled. Heart cutouts form small handles. A coat of clear finish protects the artwork from childhood spills.

MOTHER GOOSE DESIGNS

Mother Goose Quilt

Shown on pages 68-69.

Finished size is 46x46 inches.

MATERIALS
¾ yard of 45-inch wide
    unbleached muslin
1 yard of purple and pink calico
1 yard of pink pindot cotton
¼ yard of purple pindot cotton
2¾ yards of pink plaid for
    backing and nine patch
    squares
Quilt batting
Fabric paints
Dressmaker's carbon paper and
    tracing wheel
Permanent fine-tip brown
    marking pen
Graph paper
Water-erasable pen
Embroidery floss, ribbons,
    artificial flowers, pom-poms,
    and purchased appliqués to
    embellish designs
Purple pearl cotton
Embroidery hoop

INSTRUCTIONS
   Note: All measurements allow
for ¼-inch seam allowance.

For the nursery rhyme blocks
   With water erasable pen, draw
6 blocks onto the unbleached
muslin, *each* measuring 6½x6½
inches, and one block measuring
18½x18½ inches. Do not cut out.
   Enlarge the Mother Goose design, *right, above,* and the six figures, page 75, onto graph paper.
Center and transfer the drawings
to the fabric blocks using carbon
paper and tracing wheel. Trace
over the design lines with brown
marking pen.
   Complete all painting and decorative stitching before cutting out
the blocks. (For painting tips, see
page 79.) Use simple embroidery
to highlight the designs. For best
results, limit the embellishments
to details such as flowers and facial features. Trim the designs
with pom-poms, flowers, ribbons,
and purchased appliqués. Cut
blocks from fabric; set aside.

1 Square = 1 Inch

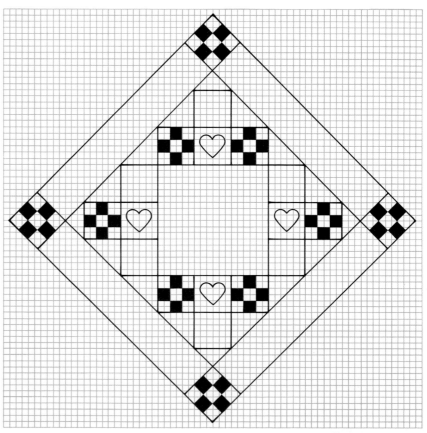

1 Square = 1 Inch

Quilt – 1 Square = ½ Inch   Pillow – 1 Square = 1 Inch

For the appliquéd heart blocks

Cut four blocks from the calico to measure 6½x6½ inches. Make a heart-shaped template from the cardboard to fit the square. Add ¼-inch seam allowance and cut four hearts from the pink pindot fabric. Baste and press under raw edges of hearts and appliqué to the calico blocks.

For the nine-patch blocks

Make a square cardboard template measuring 2½x2½ inches. Cut 40 blocks from *each* of the purple pindot and the plaid fabrics. Cut 10 blocks from the pink pindot fabric. Referring to the photograph, pages 68-69, for placement, piece 10 nine-patch blocks; set aside.

For the triangle shapes

Draw a square measuring 6x6 inches. Draw an X through the square. Cut large triangle (half of the square) for large pattern. Cut remaining triangle in half to make the smaller pattern. Make cardboard templates from these patterns, adding ¼-inch seam allowances to all sides. From the calico, cut 12 large triangles and 4 small triangles.

For the sashing strips

From the pink pindot fabric, cut four strips, each measuring 6½x34½ inches. With the water-erasable pen, write across the strips the following: "Old Mother Goose when" (first strip); "She wanted to wander," (second strip); "Would ride through the *continued* air" (third strip); "On a very fine gander" (fourth strip). Using the purple pearl cotton and outline stitches, embroider the strips.

Assembly of quilt top

Refer to the diagram, page 74, for the placement and order of the squares around the Mother Goose block. Noting the vertical direction of the quilt top, assemble 2 strips, *each* with one heart block between 2 nine-patch blocks and 2 more strips with one heart block between two nursery rhyme blocks. Sew one large triangle to left side of *each* of the four strips.

Sew the strips to the center block, leaving the triangle piece free on the first strip. Working *clockwise* around center block, sew the remaining strips. Sew the free edge of the triangle piece to the last 6-inch block.

Assemble 2 strips, *each* with two large triangles between one nursery rhyme block and 2 more strips with two large triangles between one nine-patch square. Piece these strips to the quilt top. Piece the four small triangles to the quilt top to complete the center square.

Piece a nine-patch square to left side of each of the sashing strips; sew strips around center square.

Finishing the quilt

From the pink plaid, cut and piece a square to measure 47x47 inches. Place batting between the quilt backing, wrong side up, and quilt top, right side up. Baste all layers together.

Machine-quilt around border design of Mother Goose block, in seam line between Mother Goose block and 6-inch blocks, in seam line around sashing strips, and around appliqué hearts.

Tie the quilt on plaid side at intersections of blocks and triangles with pearl cotton. Trim the backing to size of quilt top.

For the binding, piece 4 calico strips to measure 1½x47 inches. With right sides facing, sew strips to quilt top. Press under the raw edges and hand-sew on seam line on plaid side; finish corners.

Child's Pinafore and Bib Overalls

Shown on page 70.

MATERIALS
Purchased commercial pattern
Fabric yardage and notions specified for pattern
Graph paper; water-erasable pen
Dressmaker's carbon paper and tracing wheel
Permanent fine-tip brown marking pen; fabric paints
Embroidery floss and ribbons

INSTRUCTIONS

The painted portions of the children's clothing, page 70, are made from unbleached muslin. For best results, use 100 percent cottons when using fabric paints.

Before beginning assembly of garment, select nursery rhyme design, page 75. Decide where you want the design on the garment and cut out the pattern piece (yoke, bib, pocket, or skirt).

Trace outline of pattern piece onto fabric with water-erasable pen. Paint design on fabric before cutting out. Refer to the instructions on the quilt, page 74 (For the nursery rhyme blocks), for details on the tracing, painting, and embellishing of the design. Assemble garment according to the pattern instructions.

Old Woman in the Shoe Pull Toy

Shown on page 71.

Toy stands 13½ inches tall.

MATERIALS
2 feet of 1x12-inch clear pine
1½ feet of ½x12-inch clear pine
Scraps of 1⅛-inch clear pine
Two ¼x4⅝-inch dowels
Four ¼-inch steel washers
Two 2-inch No. 10 wood screws
One screw eye
Woodburner; acrylic paints
Cord and wooden bead for pull
Graph paper; carbon paper
Danish oil

INSTRUCTIONS

For the top

Cut two pieces of pine, each 12x12 inches from the 1-inch pine and one from the ½-inch pine. Laminate the three pieces together with the ½-inch piece placed between the two 1-inch pieces; let dry. Enlarge shape, *below,* and trace it onto the glued piece of wood; cut out with band saw and sand smooth.

Enlarge Old Woman in the Shoe pattern, *opposite,* excluding borders, onto graph paper and trace onto the shaped wood using carbon paper; flop pattern and repeat on other side.

Woodburn over traced lines and woodburn pindots evenly spaced around the shaped edges.

With acrylic paints, color design as desired. Speckle the side edges with the flower motif in the old woman's dress, using the pindots as flower centers.

For the base

From 1⅛-inch pine cut piece to measure 3½x13 inches. Drill ¼-inch holes through the center of the base 2¼ inches from each end; sand all sides.

With band saw, cut 4 wheels, each 2⅜-inch diameter; drill ¼-inch holes in the centers; sand. Run dowels through the base, place washers at ends, glue the wheels to dowel strips; sand.

Woodburn and paint a floral motif on each wheel. Repeat the floral design used on the shaped edges of the top piece around the edges of the base.

Center and glue top of toy to

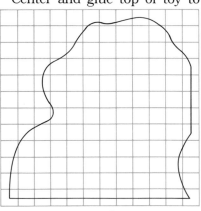

1 Square = 1 Inch

base. Secure the two pieces on underside of base with the wood screws. Attach screw eye to front of toy and add cord. Fasten a wooden bead to end of cord for pull. Rub toy with Danish oil.

Diaper Tote Bag

Shown on page 71.

Finished size is 16x18 inches.

MATERIALS
2½ yards white cotton fabric
½ yard calico for piping and
   lining handles
Scraps of fabrics for appliqués
8½ yards of cotton cording
1½ yards polyester fleece
Water-erasable pen

INSTRUCTIONS
Note: All stitching allows for a ½-inch seam allowance.

Cover the cording with bias-cut 1-inch-wide calico strips for piping; set aside.

For the pocket
Machine- or hand-appliqué your choice of design 1½ inches from the corner of a piece of white fabric cut to measure 14x16 inches. (Project bag has the flower motif from the corner of the Mother Goose block, page 74, as the appliqué design.)

Cut and baste a 14x16-inch piece of fleece to the wrong side of the appliqué block. With water-erasable pen, draw diagonal lines in two directions ¾ inch apart (to create diamonds) across the block and quilt either by hand or machine. Cut the quilted piece to measure 13x15 inches.

Baste piping around all edges and finish the joining ends. From white fabric, cut lining 13x15 inches. With right sides facing, sew the lining to the quilted piece, leaving an opening for turning; clip curves, turn, press, and sew the opening closed.

For the bag
Cut 6 rectangles, each measuring 17x19 inches—4 from the white fabric for the front and back sections and lining, 2 from the fleece. For the boxing strip, cut 2 pieces of white fabric and 1 of fleece to measure 51x5 inches.

For the handles, cut 2 pieces of white cotton, 2 pieces of fleece, and 2 pieces of calico, all to measure 20x3 inches.

Baste fleece to bag front, back, boxing strip, and handles. Sew piping to bag front and back on seam line along sides and bottom of bag; clip corners. Sew piping to sides of handles.

With right sides facing, sew calico lining to the handles on long sides; leave short ends open for turning; turn, press.

Center and baste the pocket on the front side of bag. Sew in the groove between the piping and pocket.

Sew boxing strip, right sides facing, to bag front. Sew other side of boxing strip to bag back. Clip curves, turn. Sew piping to top of bag.

Mark placement of handles at top, 2 inches from sides on bag front and back. Sew on handles; press seam allowance to inside of bag.

Assemble bag lining as for right side eliminating the piping instructions. Press under ½-inch seam allowance at top. Pin lining to the bag with handles upward. Stitch on right side of bag on the piping groove through the top of lining; press.

Wee Willie Bread-Dough Wall Plaque

Shown on page 72.

Finished plaque is 9 inches tall.

MATERIALS
1 cup flour; ¼ cup salt
⅜ cup lukewarm water
1 hairpin for hanging
Acrylic paints
Watercolor paint brushes
High-gloss polymer sealer
India ink; fine-tip pen
Small paper clip; scrap of
   leather

1 Square = 1 Inch

continued

MOTHER GOOSE DESIGNS

INSTRUCTIONS

Mix the water and salt in bowl. Add flour and mix well. If dough is stiff, add more water; if dough is sticky, add flour. Knead the dough until smooth. Shape into ball, cover, and set aside.

Enlarge the pattern of Wee Willie, page 75, onto graph paper. In order to make the design 9 inches high, chart the pattern so one square equals ¾ inch.

Lay the design on a cookie sheet covered with aluminum foil and begin to shape pieces of dough to fit over the segments of the design. Fold and crease dough to obtain realistic effects. Use water sparingly to glue pieces together as you assemble the shapes.

Begin by shaping the gown from one ball of dough; make arms and hands from separate balls and attach to gown; add head (place hairpin in back of head), then cap. Attach pajama legs under the gown, then add his ankles and slippers. Push dough through a garlic press for tassels and hair. Add collar and bow. Gently lift the pattern from the cookie sheet.

Lay a pencil in the left hand and press to make a crease for the lantern to hang over; remove pencil. Shape the lantern and place the paper clip on top for hanger. Do not place the lantern over the hand at this time.

Bake in slow oven (200 to 225 degrees) for 12 hours. Allow the shape to cool and paint as desired with acrylics, using the photograph, page 72, as a guide. When paint is dry, add facial features with the India ink and the fine-tip pen. Apply one coat of sealer and let dry.

Thread a narrow strip of leather through the paper clip on the lantern and staple the ends. Slip lantern over Wee Willie's hand.

Wooden Toy Box

Shown on page 72.

The finished size of the box is 24x17½ inches.

MATERIALS

6 pieces of 1x6x26-inch clear pine for ends
4 pieces of 1x10x18-inch clear pine for sides
1 piece of 14½x16-inches plywood for bottom
6d finishing nails
Sixteen ⅜x1½-inch dowel pins
Wood glue; graph paper
Woodburning tool; satin-finish polyurethane varnish

INSTRUCTIONS

For the end pieces

(Make 2.) Glue and dowel-joint 3 pieces of wood together.

For the side pieces

(Make 2.) Glue and dowel-joint 2 pieces of wood together.

Clamp and let the dowel-joint pieces of wood set overnight. Sand smoothly on all sides.

For the box assembly

Enlarge the box patterns, *right*, onto graph paper and trace outline onto the appropriate wood pieces. (On the end pieces, the grain of wood runs vertically; on side pieces, the grain runs horizontally.) Cut out shapes from the wood. On the 2 end pieces, trace the heart design; use jigsaw to cut out.

Glue and nail front and back to the end pieces. Sand. Glue and nail the bottom of box in place.

For the woodburning

Enlarge four nursery rhyme designs, pages 74, 77, and 79, onto graph paper. With carbon paper, transfer one design to each side of box. Use the flower motif in the border design around the curved sides of the heart. Wood-burn over the traced lines. Finish with coat of varnish.

Mother Goose Pillows

Shown on page 73.

The finished size of Wee Willie Winkie is 14x11 inches. Little Bo Peep is 13½x10½ inches.

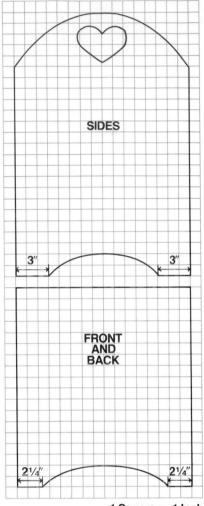

1 Square = 1 Inch

MATERIALS

½ yard unbleached cotton muslin
½ yard calico for piping and back
Graph paper
1 yard of narrow cotton cord for piping or narrow lace trim for edging
Dressmaker's carbon paper and tracing wheel
Permanent fine-tip brown marking pen
Acrylic or fabric paints
Sable paintbrush
Embroidery floss, pearl cottons, pom-poms, rickrack, ribbons, artificial flowers, and flower appliqués for embellishments
Embroidery hoop and needle
Polyester fiberfill

INSTRUCTIONS

Enlarge patterns onto graph paper. Double the size of the pattern by letting one square equal 2

1 Square = 1 Inch

1 Square = 1 Inch

inches in order to obtain the pillow measurements. Transfer the design to fabric using dressmaker's carbon and tracing wheel.

On the right side, trace the lines with a brown marking pen.

For decorating the pillow top

Complete all painting and decorative stitching before cutting out the fabric shapes.

Place a small amount of paint on a glass plate and thin with a few drops of water until the paint is of light-cream consistency.

To prevent paint from bleeding on the fabric, do not overload the brush. Paint up to but not over the brown outlines. Leave a sliver of unpainted fabric between colors to keep them from running together. Paint large areas of color first, letting each painted area dry before moving on to the next area.

If you make a mistake, dab at the paint with a wet tissue. If this does not remove the error, brush a bit of white paint over the mistake; when dry, paint the correct color on top.

When paint is dry, set the colors by pressing the wrong side of the fabric with a warm iron. Spray-starch the fabric lightly as you press to give it extra body.

Use simple embroidery stitches to highlight the design. For best results, limit the embellishments to the important details such as trims, flowers, and facial features. Trim the designs with rickrack, pom-poms, flowers, ribbon bows, purchased appliqués, or beads.

For sewing the pillow

Draw a stitching line ¾ inch beyond design shape on top and sides. Draw a straight line across bottom.

Cut calico or muslin fabric the size of front piece for backing. Cover cording with bias-cut calico fabric to make piping trim as on Wee Willie pillow or use narrow lace in lieu of piping. Stitch trim on marked stitching line.

With right sides of back and front together, sew on stitching line, leaving an opening at bottom. Trim seams, clip curves and corners; turn, stuff firmly. Slip-stitch the opening closed.

ACKNOWLEDGMENTS

Our special thanks to the following designers who contributed projects to this book. When more than one project appears on a page, the acknowledgment specifically cites the project with the page number. A page number alone indicates one designer or source has contributed all of the project material listed for that page.

Amy Albert—21, bluebird
Linda Armentrout—72, dough hanger
David Ashe—62, puzzle
Mary Lamb Becker—61, bear's sweater, cap, and scarf
Marlaine Beeble—37
Coats & Clark—30-31; 32-33; 34-35
Laura Holtorf Collins—4-5; 68-69, quilt design
The Design Concern—7, wood blocks
Susan Douglas—36
Phyllis Dunstan—9, bonnet; 22, cottage music box
Dixie Falls—8
Debra Felton—63, adaptation of cross-stitched bears
Folkwear Patterns—9, christening gown
Ron Hawbaker—72, toy box
Diane Hayes—20, album cover; 60, appliqué stocking
Chris Kinka—52
Alla Ladyzhensky—23, sampler

Lyn Lidsky—62-63, appliqué bears
Carol Lisbona—62-63, dough ornaments
Donna Martin—61, bear
Sally Mavor—20-21, baby bibs
Janet McCafferty—68-69, Mother Goose designs
Jean Norman—7, smocked bib
Jan Peterson—21, clown block
Charlene Pulliam—22, gift bags
Beverly Rivers—48-49; 51
Gene Rosenberg—6
Mimi Shimmin—53
Viking Sewing Machine—50
Don Wipperman—71, pull toy

For their cooperation and courtesy, we extend a special thanks to the following sources:

Coats & Clark, Inc.
    72 Cummings Point Road
    Stamford, CT 06902
DMC Corporation
    197 Trumbull Street
    Elizabeth, NJ 07206
Folkwear
    Box 3798
    San Rafael, CA 94912
C.M. Offray & Son, Inc.
    261 Madison Ave.
    New York, NY 10016

A special thank-you to the following persons whose skills and efforts are greatly appreciated.

Eleanor Rinehart
Margaret Sindelar
Clara Storm

We also are pleased to acknowledge the following photographers, whose talents and technical skills contributed much to this book.

Mike Dieter—4-5; 7, smocked bib; 9; 20-21; 22-23; 53
Hedrich-Blessing—6; 7, blocks; 8; 24-25; 30-31; 32-33; 34-35; 36; 48-49; 50-51
Hopkins Associates—37; 52; 60-61; 62-63; 68-69; 70-71; 72-73
Scott Little—52; 62, tree puzzle